# Kinetic Konnections

## ~The Poetry We Live~

Kumudini Ved

AF520115

BookMyStory®

Kinetic Konnections
The Poetry We Live
Kumudini Ved

Published in 2026



© Published by

BookMyStory®

*It's time you tell your story*

BookMyStory
Thane, 400615, India
info@bookmystorypublishing.com
www.bookmystorypublishing.com



ISBN: 978-93-49509-53-5 Multiple Languages [Paperback / softback]

Cover Sketch by Kumudini Ved
Editorial Consulting by Neha Ved Worddpreneur®
Book Curated and supported by PenVmedia®

# *Gratitude*

This book is the culmination of a journey that began decades ago, a journey of words, wonder, and unwavering belief.

My deepest gratitude goes to my third standard teacher, Ms. Brown, who handed us our first creative writing assignment and unknowingly handed me my lifelong purpose. I still remember choosing to write about Sunset, and how she showed us that a handful of carefully chosen words could build a world. That tiny exercise became the first brick in the home I would someday build with poetry.

To all my teachers, in school and college...who shaped my expression, refined my language, and nurtured every story, poem, and essay I attempted: I am fortunate to have had mentors who saw beyond the student and encouraged the writer in me.

To my father, Ramniklal Kalyanji...my first guide in literature and language. He filled our home with Shakespearean verses, folk songs and poetry from various ages he could quote verbatim, classical works, and a love for beautifully crafted thought. His passion became my foundation.

To my mother, Indumati Ramniklal, I remember singing with you, not for an audience, but simply because harmony made us feel whole. Those melodies stitched confidence into my voice and love into my words.

To my husband, Dr Paresh... who stood beside me through the many years when responsibilities demanded more than dreams dared. We've braved the high and lows together. Thank you for your resilience and being a true family man.

To my daughter, Neha... who witnessed this dream unfold quietly from the sidelines, who observed, understood, and encouraged without ever demanding. Thank you for knowing how much this means to me. You are one of my greatest reasons to shine. And thank you to your team at PenVmedia for being an organised workforce that brought the abstract to life.

To my son-in-law, Vicky... for becoming not just a part of our family, but a quiet strength within it. His calm presence, steady support, and gentle respect for my creative world have meant more than words can express.

To my son, Rahul...whose vociferous attitude keeps me on my toes with a constant reminder that dreams don't come with an expiry date, but goals need a deadline to be achieved. Thank you for keeping my heart young and thumping.

To Utsavi... the daughter I gained by her marriage to Rahul. You have been my artistic companion and fuelled my creative energy. Thank you for your warmth, support and adding more love to this family.

To my granddaughter Tiana... whose laughter is pure poetry... thank you for bringing colours that even my imagination had not discovered and for giving my second innings a purpose.

A heartfelt tribute to my manasi (ordained by heart) guru, Gulzar Saab, the poet whose words taught my feelings how to take form in writing. From the moment I first heard "Koi Hota Jisko Apna..." as a nine-year-old, to today, his poetry has been my guiding lantern. Somewhere, in the quiet between his lines, I found the courage to write my own.

Finally, my thanks to every reader who holds this book today: Thank you for becoming part of the poetry I live.

Love Always,

Kumudini Ved

# Table of Contents

# *Poems in Hindi*

# माँ

माँ, माई, आई, दोस्त, तेरे अनेक नाम!
तूने दिया जीवन को श्वास, काया को जीवन, और इस आत्मा को एक मुकाम !
मेरे पिता के सपनों की ताकत हो तुम, इस मकान को घर बनाने का अटूट जोड हो तुम!
अक्सर, हमारे सपने पूरे करते-करने, तूने अपने सपनों को जिंदा जला दिया!
फिर भी, हमें अपनी खुशी के आसमान पर उड़ते देख, मुस्कुराकर अपना आँचल लेहरा दिया।
तुम हो तो, इस जहाँ को हम देख पाये...
माँ तुम एक गेहरा ऐहसास हो जो धड़कन में रहती हो,
इक शबनमी, मरमरी, सुकून की चद्दर हो ।
माँ तुम हर मुश्किल, संकट या कठनाई से झूंझकर जीतने का त्यौहार हो!

# Maa

Maa, Mai, Aai, Dost, tere anek naam!
Tune diya jeevan ko shvaas, kaya ko jeevan - aur is aatma ko ek mukaam!
Mere pita ke sapno ki taakat ho tum, is makaan ko ghar banane ka atoot jod ho tum!
Aksar, humare sapne poore karte-karte, tune apne sapno ko zinda jala diya!
Phir bhi, humein apni khushi ke aasmaan par udte dekh, muskuraakar apna aanchal lehra diya.
Tum ho to, is jahan ko hum dekh paaye...
Maa tum ek gehra ehsaas ho jo dhadkan mein rehti ho,
Ik shabnami, marmari, sukoon ki chaddar ho!
Maa tum har mushkil, sankat ya kathinai se jhoojhkar jeetne ka tyohaar ho!

# पिता

पूर्वजों के आशिर्वाद से, पुनर जन्म की पेहली प्रतिष्ठित साँस से लेकर;
हमारी हर आयु हर उम्मीद, हर मांग, हर सपने में हमेशा शामिल रहता है
जो जीवन के उतार-चढ़ाव,
परिस्थिती विपरीत हो तो, हमारे हौसलों को अपनी स्थिरता के स्पर्श से सहलाएं,
ना गवारा को भी अच्छा, और ना खुश को भी खुश सर्जाता...
वो है Dad - पिता!
कदम-कदम, हमारे धड़कते दिल की धड़कन है... Dad - पिता!
जब भी साँसे ख़त्म हो, नब्ज़ हो रुकी,
जब सुलगती हो उसकी चिता, फिर भी उसके
होने का जो एहसास दिलाता है वो है... Dad - पिता!

# Pita

Poorvajon ke aashirvaad se, punar janm ki pehli pratishthit
saans se lekar;
Hamari har aayu har umgid, har maang, har sapne mein
hamesha shaamil rehta hai jo
Jeevan ke utaar-chadhaav, paristhiti vipreet ho to, hamare
hoslon ko apni sthirta ke sparsh se sailaaye
Na gavaara ko bhi accha, aur na khush ko bhi khush kar jaata,
wo hai Dad - Pita
Kadam-kadam, hamare dhadakte dil ki dhadkan hai Dad -
Pita!
Jab bhi saanse khatam ho, nabz ho ruki,
Jab sulagti ho uski chita, phir bhi uske
hone ka jo ehsas dilata hai wo hai ek, Dad, Pita!

# हम लेखक है

हम लेखक है
शब्दों का ताना-बाना बुनकर सपनों की दुनियाँ सजाते हैं।
हक़ीकत के धुंधले कोहरे से निकल,
ख़यालों की उजली, झिलमिलाती हुई सतरंगी तस्वीर बनाते हैं।
कहानियाँ, निबंध, उपन्यास, नज़म, बज़म गज़ल और कविताओं का
साम्राज्य है हम लेखकों का।
कल्पना शक्ति, सुंदर बोल, तीखा कटाक्श, सत्य वचन
और आत्मविश्वास ही हमारे हर सोच का भन्डार है।
हम लेखकों को ही मिला है यह वरदान, जहाँ पर कोई व्यक्ति या सोच न
पहुँचे, हमारी कलम पहुँचे वहाँ।
जहाँ न पहुँचे सूरज की उजली किरणें, हमारी कलम पहुँचे वहाँ।
जहाँ न पहुँचे कलात्मकता, हमारी कलम पहुँचे वहाँ।

# Hum Lekhak Hai

Hum lekhak hai
Shabdon ka taana-baana bunkar sapnon ki duniya sajaate hain.
Haqeeqat ke dhundhle kohre se nikal,
Khayalon ki ujli, jhilmilaati hui satrangi tasveer banaate hain.
Kahaniyan, nibandh, upanyaas, nazm, bazm ghazal aur
kavitaon ka saamrajya hai hum lekhakon ka.
Kalpana shakti, sundar bol, teekha kataaksh, satya vachan
Aur aatmavishvaas hi hamaare har soch ka bhandaar hai.
Hum lekhakon ko hi mila hai yeh vardaan, jahan par koi
vyakti ya soch na pahunche, hamaari kalam pahunche wahan.
Jahan na pahunche sooraj ki ujli kiranen, hamaari kalam
pahunche wahan.
Jahan na pahunche kalaatmakta, hamaari kalam pahunche
wahan.

# बंद दरवाज़ा

समय बीत जाए तो मौकों के लिए दरवाज़े बंद हो जाते हैं।
उम्र निकल जाए तो रास्ते तय करने के
बुलन्द इरादों के दरवाज़े बंद हो जाते हैं।
दिलों से विश्वास उठ जाए तो,
सब रिश्ते-नातों कि सुहानी रजाई ओढने के
अवसर बन्द हो जाते हैं।
मगर ऐ दिल, तू ना गभरा, जहाँ में एक दरवाज़ा बंद हो तो,
दस दरीचे और कई दिवारें हट जाती है।
संझेले अपने मन में ये भरोसा, कि हर
पतझड़ के बाद वसंत ज़रुर आती है,
हर गहरी खाई से, अँधेरे के बाद, सुनहेरी उशा मुस्कुराती है
हर रुदन भरी तृष्णा के बाद, आत्माँ तृप्ती-सुधा की खुली श्वास,
ज़रूर पाती है।

# Band Darwaja

Samay beet jaaye to maukon ke liye darwaaze band ho jaate hain.
Umr nikal jaaye to raaste tay karne ke
Buland iraadon ke darwaaze band ho jaate hain.
Dilon se vishvaas uth jaaye to,
Sab rishte-naaton ki suhaani rajaai odhne ke
Avsar band ho jaate hain.
Magar ai dil, tu na ghabra, jahan mein ek darwaaza band ho to,
Das dariche aur kai deewaaren hat jaati hain.
Sanjhele apne man mein yeh bharosa, ki har
Patjhad ke baad vasant zarur aati hai,
Har gehri khaai se, andhere ke baad sunehri usha muskuraati hai.
Ghar rudan bhari trishna ke baad, aatmaon tripti-sudha ki khuli shwaas, zarur paati hai.

# निशित का तिमिर-उर्फ रातका अंधकार!

सूरज धलते-धलते अपनी  लालिमाँ की आभा को क्षितिज पर गुलाल की
तरह उड़ाता  चला है।
चहकते-लेहकते पंछी अपने आशियाँने की ओर उड़ते चले आ रहे हैं।
टिलों से उतरती गैया के गले की घंटी
मानो संधर्याती गाती है।
और इनके कदमों के तले उड़ती गोधुली,
मानो धरती को चंदन का तिलक कर रही हो।
दूर कहीं छोटी पहाड़ी पर उमड़ते अंधकार में लुप्त होता शिव मंदिर के
कलश का त्रिशूल...
वहाँ वादी में गूंजता शंख और घंटनाद,
रात की सियाही का मानो आगमन कर रहा है ।
जीवन की सुविधाएँ  जुटाने है की आपा-धापी
हड्डी-पसली निचोड़ के रख देने वाली भीड़-भाड़,
गंदगी, रोग, झुग्गी-झोपड़ी;
इस कोलाहल के बीच शीशे के माचिस के डिब्बों
जैसी अनगिनत मंज़िला इमारतें
मानो कोई काँच और लोहे से बने पत्थर की आँख वाले, निगरानी रखने
संतरी हैं।
इन सब से दिन भर झुजकर लौटता मानव समुदाय,
अपनी गर्म छत्त के नीचे, सुरक्षित्ता की नरम चादर ओढ़कर सो रहा है।
जैसे असंख्य सुर्ख नज़ारों को और सिसकते संनाटों को,
रात अपनी काली, गेहरी, खाई जैसे आँचल में समेट लेती है।
मानो जैसे, जन्म हो या मरण,
कत्ल हो या शहादत, खुशियां या घातकी ज़ख्म,
सब पर एक, तारों से टिमटिमाता काला कफ़न ओढ़ा देती है |

# Nishit Ka Timir – Urf Raat ka Andhakaar!

Sooraj dhalte-dhalte apni laalimaã ki aabha ko kshitij par
gulaal ki tarah udaata chala hai.
Chahakte-lehakte panchhi apne aashiyaane ki or udte chale
aa rahe hain.
Tilon se utarti gaiya ke gale ki ghanti
Maano sandharyaati gaati hai.
Aur inke kadmon ke tale udti godhooli,
Maano dharti ko chandan ka tilak kar rahi ho.
Door kahin chhoti pahaadi par umadte andhakaar mein lupt
hota Shiv mandir ke kalash ka trishool...
Wahan vaadi mein goonjta shankh aur ghantnaad,
Raat ki siyaahi ka maano aagaman kar raha hai.
Jeevan ki suvidhaaye jutaane ki aapa-dhaapi,
Haddi-pasli nichod ke rakh dene wali bheed-bhaad,
Gandagi, rog, jhuggi-jhopdi;
Is kolaahal ke beech sheeshe ke maachis ke dibbon
Jaisi anginat manzila imaarate
Maano koi kaanch aur lohe se bane patthar ki aankh wale,
nigrani rakhne santari hain.
In sab se din bhar jhujhkar lautta maanav samudaay,
Apni garam chhat ke neeche, surakshitta ki naram chaadar
odhkar so raha hai.
Jaise asankhya surkh nazaaron ko aur sisakte sannaaton ko,
Raat apni kaali, gehri, khaai jaise aanchal mein samet leti hai.
Maano jaise, janm ho ya maran,
Qatl ho ya shahaadat, khushiyaan ya ghaatki zakhm,
Sab par ek, taaron se timtimaata kaala kafan odha deti hai.

# उम्मीद की दुकान

हर शाम ढलता  सूरज जीवन की थकान,
अपूर्णता और सवालों की अपनी काली,
मखमली राजाई ओढाकर जाता है।
हर सुबह फिर से सूरज नई उमीद, हर्ष और
हौसले से भरी अपनी मुस्कान लिए  उभरता है।
हर रोज उगते सूरज के साथ, उत्तम चाचा,
अपना इक्कीस  कलिदार, नवरंगी, गोल, गुंबजी
छाता खिलोने से लाद कर निकल पड़ते ।
लंबे-चैडे भारी लकड़ी के स्थम्भ पर उनकी
विशाल छतरी को है टिकाते।
चमकिले कपड़ो में सजे, गुड्डा-गुड़ियाँ,
चाबिवाला बंदर- भालू, छोटा प्लेन, हेलिकोपटर
गाड़ी, रेलगाड़ी,  काँच के कंचों की पोटलियाँ,
कागज की पवन चकियाँ, पीतल के गुंगरू, ओम और त्रिशूल से सुजे सजे
चाबियों के छल्ले, छोटे बड़े लट्टू और अनगिनत खिलोनों से उनके दाएं
कांधे पर टिकी विशाल छतरीली दुकान सजती।
उन्की एक पुकार, "खिलोने ले लो, खिलोने" और उनकी तीर सी चीरती
सीटी को सुन के, सब बच्चे और अनेक बुज़र्ग उन्हें घेर लेते।
कोई लकडी के, कोई रुई के कोई रेशम के, तो कोई मिट्टी के...
हर कोई अपने प्यारे, चहिते खिलोने खरिद ते
क्यों कि ये सिर्फ खिलोने नहीं... उम्मीद, खुशी, और सपने बाँटते,
तभी तो ये उम्मीद चाचा खिलेने वाले कहलाते |

# Umeed Ki Dukaan

Har shaam dhalta sooraj jeevan ki thakaan,
Apoornata aur sawaalon ki apni kaali,
Makhmali rajaai odhaakar jaata hai.
Har subah phir se sooraj nayi umeed, harsh aur
Hausle se bhari apni muskaan liye ubharta hai.
Har roz ugte sooraj ke saath, Uttam chacha,
Apna ikkees kalidaar, navrangi, gol, gumbaji
Chhaata khilonon se laad kar nikal padte.
Lambe-chaude bhaari lakdi ke stambh par unki
Vishaal chhatri ko hai tikaate.
Chamakile kapdon mein saje, gudda-gudiyan,
Chaabiwala bandar-bhaalu, chhota plane, helicopter,
Gaadi, railgaadi, kaanch ke kanchon ki potliyaan,
Kaagaz ki pavan chakkiyaan, peetal ke gungroo,
Om aur trishool se suse saje chaabiyon ke chhalle,
Chhote-bade latttoo aur anginat khilonon se
Unke daayein kandhe par tiki vishaal chhatreeli dukaan sajti.
Unki ek pukaar, “Khilone le lo, khilone”
Aur unki teer si cheerti seeti ko sun ke,
Sab bachche aur anek buzurg unhein gher lete.
Koi lakdi ke, koi rui ke, koi resham ke,
To koi mitti ke...
Har koi apne pyaare, chahite khilone kharidte,
Kyonki yeh sirf khilone nahin... umeed, khushi aur sapne baantte,
Tabhi to yeh Umeed Chacha Khilonewala kehlaate.

# एक खत ज़िंदगी के नाम

हाँ, माँ की कोख से निकलकर धरती पर पहली साँस लेने का रास्ता
आसान नहीं।
हाँ एक मुट्ठी जितने चुझे का बड़ी मुरगी बनने का सफर आसान नहीं।
एक छोटे से हिरण के बच्चे को पूरा 600 kg का बारा सिंगा बन्ने का
मुकाम, आसानी से मिलता नहीं।
ज़िन्दगी, हर जीव से तूम उस्के हिस्से की कड़ी मेहनत वसूल करती हो।
कली को सूर्य किरण में तप कर खुद को खिलाने का ज़िम्मा देती हो।
बीज को मिट्टी की गहराई में अपने जड़ फ़ैलाने, और धरा पर अपना धड
उगाने का कष्ट करवाती हो।
मनुष्य को पेहली हसी से लेकर उनके उतार-चडाव की लेहरों पर डोलती
जीवन नैयाँ को स्थिर रखने का संघर्ष करवाती हो।
उम्र के हर पडाव पर, आशाओं-निराशाओं के मेले में,
सफलता असफलता के झमेले में,
नीती अनीती के चैराहों पर, सब परिस्थिति में, हमसे जी तोड परिश्रम
करवाती हो।
फिर भी जिंदगी तूम खूबसूरत, लाजवाब,
आकर्षित और वरदान रूपीनी हो।
ए जिंदगी मुझे तुमपर नाज़ है, बेपन्हा प्यार है, और भरोसा है।

# Ek Khat Zindagi Ke Naam

Haan, maa ki kokh se nikal kar dharti par pehli saans lene ka raasta aasaan nahin.
Haan, ek muddhi jitne chuje ka badi murgi banne ka safar aasaan nahin.
Ek chhote se hiran ke bachche ko poora 600 kg ka baara singa banne ka mukaam, aasaani se milta nahin.
Zindagi, har jeev se tum uske hisse ki kadi mehnat vasool karti ho.
Kali ko soorya kiran mein tap kar khud ko khilaane ka zimma deti ho.
Beej ko mitti ki gehraai mein apni jad phailaane, aur dhara par apna dhad ugaane ka kasht karvaati ho.
Manushya ko pehli hasi se lekar unke utaar-chadhaav ki lehron par dolti jeevan naiya ko sthir rakhne ka sangharsh karvaati ho.
Umr ke har padaav par, aashaon-niraashaon ke mele mein,
Safalta-asafalta ke jhamele mein,
Neeti-aneeti ke chaurahon par, sab paristhitiyon mein, humse jee tod parishram karvaati ho.
Phir bhi zindagi tum khoobsurat, laajavaab, aakarshit aur vardaan roopini ho.
Ae zindagi, mujhe tumpar naaz hai, bepanah pyaar hai, aur bharosa hai.

# अब की बार जब जाओगे

अब की बार जब अपने सपने को साकार करने के लिए जाओगे,
तो खुद के होस्ले पर भरोसा रखना।
डटे रहना, तब तक, जब तक,
जिन्दगी तेरा इम्तेहान लेते-लेले थके नहीं !
मेहनत, लगन, हिम्मत, ज्ञान जो कुछ लगे
वो इस बार अपनी इच्छा की भट्टी में झोंक देना
मगर हासिल कर लेना अपनी मंज़िल;
और साकार कर लेना अपना जीना !

# Ab Ki Baar Jaoge

Ab ki baar jab apne sapne ko saakaar karne ke liye jaaoge,
To khud ke hausle par bharosa rakhna.
Date rehna, tab tak, jab tak,
Zindagi tera imtehaan lete-lete thak nahin jaati!
Mehnat, lagan, himmat, gyaan jo kuch lage,
Woh is baar apni ichchha ki bhatti mein jhonk dena,
Magar haasil kar lena apni manzil;
Aur saakaar kar lena apna jeena!

# लोकडाउन के फौजी

लोकडाऊन में हो कोविड, या कोविड से हो लाकडाउन !
शहर हो या गाँव, हम भी भारत माँ के फौजी हैं।
हर मकान की नीव में हम, हर पुल के मज़बूत स्तम्भ में हम, हर बिजली
की तार में हम।
हर कारखने, दफतर में हम ।
दुकान, अस्पताल, पढ़ाई, विज्ञान, कला में
हम खेतों खलियाँनों में खादि-रेशम, रंगो, पटाखों,
और पतंग में हम।
शान्ती का समय हो या आपातकाल, हम भी तीनों सेना की बाहु बल
बन्कर देश की सेवा में आगे चलते हैं ।
हम श्रमिक, हम मज़दूर, हम देश की प्रगती की रीड की हड्डी है ।
हम भी फौजी, इस भारत माँ के हैं।

# Lockdown Ke Fauji

Lokdown mein ho Covid, ya Covid se ho lockdown!
Shehar ho ya gaon, hum bhi Bharat Maa ke fauji hain.
Har makaan ki neev mein hum, har pul ke mazboot stambh
mein hum, har bijli ki taar mein hum.
Har kaarkhane, daftar mein hum.
Dukaan, aspataal, padhai, vigyaan, kala mein
Hum kheton-khalihanon mein, khaad-resham, rangon,
patakhon,
Aur patang mein hum.
Shaanti ka samay ho ya aapaatkaal, hum bhi teeno sena ki
baahu-bal bankar desh ki seva mein aage chalte hain.
Hum shramik, hum mazdoor, hum desh ki pragati ki reed ki
haddi hain.
Hum bhi fauji is Bharat Maa ke hain.

# कलाकारों के लिए कलाकार

जान है, तो जहान हैं। साँस है तो दिल धड़कता है।
तेरी मुस्कान से मेरी मुस्कान तक का हॉटलाइन है।
तू खुश, तो मैं खुश, ये अपना टैगलाइन है ।
हाथ से मिले हाथ, तो साथ को मिले साथ।
जैसे जड़ से पेड़ की ताकत है,
वैसे साथ जुड़े रहने से, हमारी बरकत है।
बिमारी, बेबसी, और बदसलूकी से हो सकते है फ्री
अगर हम, हिम्मत से, हौसलें से आगे बढ़े तो लेंगे जी।
फूल अनेक, हम मगर, गुलदस्ता खुशियों का तो एक है।
जान है तो, जहान है।
साँस है तो दिल धडकता है।

# Kalakaaro Ke Liye Kalakaar

Jaan hai, to jahaan hai. Saans hai to dil dhadakta hai.
Teri muskaan se meri muskaan tak ka hotline hai.
Tu khush, to main khush, yeh apna tagline hai.
Haath se mile haath, to saath ko mile saath.
Jaise jad se ped ki taakat hai,
Vaise ek doosre se mile rehne se, hamaari barkat hai.
Bimaari, bebasi, aur badsalooki se ho sakte hain free,
Agar hum, himmat se, hauslon se aage badhein to lenge jee.
Phool anek, hum magar, guldasta khushiyon ka to ek hai.
Jaan hai to, jahaan hai.
Saans hai to dil dhadakta hai.

# बचपन - निखालासता का गुलदस्तां

वसंत रितु में बाग-बगीचों में चहकते पंछियों के संग गाना
हज़ारों रंगीन फूलों की धरा पर बिछी इंद्रधनुषी चदरीया पे दैडना,
इमली, आम, अमरुद, बेर, काले जामुन, कच्ची
सोंफ - इस उपजाव धरती के अनगिनत उपहार से पेट पूजा करना।
एक साइकिल की अंदर की ट्यूब, एक लकड़ी की सहायता से मीलों
भागते हुए खुद, भागते जाना!
लेहरों में भिगते हुए, पत्थरों पर आगे निकल जाना।
सावन में रिम-झिम की पुहार में मन के मोर भी नाच उठता।
शीत काल में ऊनी कपड़े पहनकर, बर्फिली जील पर लेटे रहना!
मौसम बदलते गये, आँख मिचोली खेलते हुए!
उम्र ने कर्वट ली, बचपन कब जवानी की और बढ़ गया,
और जवानी कब बुढ़ापे में परिवर्तित हो गयी?
ये समय का बहाव हमें अकेला कर गया !
और बचपन की उस निखलासता का अभाव दे गया !

# Bachpan, Nikhlaasataa ka Guldasta.

Vasant ritu mein baag-bageechon mein chahakte panchhiyon
ke sang gaana,
Hazaaron rangeen phoolon ki dhara par bichhi
indradhanushi chadariya pe daudna,
Imli, aam, amrud, ber, kaale jaamun, kacchi
Saunf - is upjaav dharti ke anginat uphaar se pet pooja karna.
Ek cycle ki andar ki tube, ek lakdi ki sahaayata se meelon
bhaagte hue khud, bhaagte jaana!
Lehron mein bheegte hue, pattharon par aage nikal jaana.
Saavan mein rim-jhim ki puhaar mein man ke mor bhi naach
uthta.
Sheet kaal mein ooni kapde pehankar, barfeeli jeel par lete
rehna!
Mausam badalte gaye, aankh micholi khelte hue!
Umr ne karvat li, bachpan kab jawani ki aur badh gaya,
Aur jawani kab budhaape mein parivartit ho gayi?
Yeh samay ka bahaav humein akela kar gaya!
Aur bachpan ki us nikhaalasta ka abhaav de gaya!

# खुली आँखों के सपने

सपने अंतरआत्मा की साँस है।
जो कुछ भी हम जागते, अपनी पंचइन्द्रियों से महसूस करते हैं,
वही सपने बन नींद लूट लेते हैं
सपने अपनी अंदरूनी इच्छाएं, आशाएं,
और ज़िन्दगी की बेहतरी की ऊर्जा हैं ।
कुछ हासिल करने की प्रेरणा हैं सपने।
जो हज़ार "ना" सुन के भी, एक ही उम्मीद भरी मंज़िल,
"हाँ," की तरफ भागे,वो है सपने!
कोई साथ दे या ना... कोई संग चले, हममें विश्वास रखे या ना...
हम जीस एक धूनी में चले जाते हैं, वो प्यास है,
खुली आँख के अपने सपने।
ये तो वो मृगतृष्णा है, जिस ओर मन यूं खिंचा चला जाता है
ज्यों मधुकर कलियों की और जैसे नदियाँ सागर की और!

# Khuli Aakhon Ke Sapne

Sapne antaraatma ki saans hain.
Jo kuch bhi hum jaagte, apni panchindriyon se mehsoos karte hain, wahi sapne ban neend loot lete hain.
Sapne apni androoni ichchhaen, aashaen, aur zindagi ki behtari ki urja hain.
Kuch haasil karne ki prerana hain sapne.
Jo hazaar "na" sun ke bhi, ek hi umeed bhari manzil, "haan," ki taraf bhaage,
Woh hain sapne!
Koi saath de ya na... koi sang chale, hummein vishvaas rakhe ya na...
Hum jis ek dhuni mein chale jaate hain, woh pyaas hai, khuli aankh ke apne sapne.
Yeh to woh mriga-trishna hai, jis or mann yun khincha chala jaata hai,
Jyon madhukar kaliyon ki or, jaise nadiyaan saagar ki or!

# खत

उस दिन की तंग मुलाकात के बाद, मेरा मन बहुत त्रासित हो गया।
बहुत कुछ कहा और सुना भी, मगर मन में अब भी भार रह गया।
जैसे रेत तेजी से छूट जाती है मुट्ठी करने से
वैसे तेरा हाथ मेरे हाथ से निकले जाता है,
जितना भी मैं कसना चाहूँ जी जान से!
तेरे बिना मेरी सुबह सूनी, रातें विरान,
हर रितु नीरस, हर लम्हा बेज़ार, मेरे सपने प्यासे और परेशान
इस खत में मेरी आत्मा की पुकार लिखता हूँ।
सुनकर एक बार मिल लेना, इतनी उम्मीद रखता हूँ।
ना कह दूँ , और मुंह मोड़ लूँ
यह मुझसे न हो पाएगा, अखीर...
हाथ छूट जाने से प्यार ख़त्म नहीं हो जाता।

# Khat

Us din ki tang mulaakaat ke baad, mera mann bahut traasit ho gaya.
Bahut kuch kaha aur suna bhi, magar mann mein ab bhi bhaar reh gaya.
Jaise ret tezī se chhoot jaati hai mutthi karne se,
Vaise tera haath mere haath se nikle jaata hai,
Jitna bhi main kasna chaahoon jee jaan se!
Tere bina meri subah sooni, raatein viraan,
Har ritu neeras, har lamha bezaar, mere sapne pyaase aur pareshaan.
Is khat mein meri aatma ki pukaar likhta hoon.
Sunkar ek baar mil lena, itni umeed rakhta hoon.
Na keh doon, aur munh mod loon,
Yeh mujhse na ho paayega, aakhir...
Haath chhoot jaane se pyaar khatm nahin ho jaata.

# उम्र पचपन की, मन बचपन का

कल शाम पार्क में मैं तरुण-तरुनियों के साथ में,
बड़े चाव से लंगडी खेल रही थी!
क्योंकि, मैं हूं पचपन से परे, मन है बचपन की।
खिल-खिलाहट आँखें हैं उत्साह भरी।
दो बुजुर्ग मुझ पे चिल्लाने लगे,
"अरे शर्म कर तेरे बाल सफेद हो चले, मगर अक्कल नहीं आई?
दो चोटी करके, छोटे बच्चों जैसे कपडे पहन लेनेसे, जवानी वापस नहीं आ जाती, गिरोगी तो हड्डीया टूट जाएंगी।"
मैंने अपना खेलना रोका नहीं।
मगर घर आने के बाद, रात को बिस्तर में पड़े पड़े ये विचार आया,
उम्र मेरी कुछ भी हो, क्या मैं निर्जिव होने से पेहले ही मेरी उर्जा को मुक्त कर दूँ अपने मन से, और स्तगित कर दे अपनी कंचन काया ?
अगले दिन फिर वो दो बुजुर्ग वीले, और वही रोक-टोक का आलाप।
मैंने पलट के कहा, "चाचाजी, आप अपनी जिंदगी बरसों में गिनते रहो, मैं तो सुन्दर यादें  समेट ने में मानती हूँ
आप समय की सूईयाँ बटोरो, मैं तो हर्ष-उल्लास के खुले विचारों को लेकर, बह चली आशाओं की नदी में, जिस में आया है सैलाब!"

# Umra Pachpan Ki, Mann Bachpan Ka

Kal shaam park mein main tarun-taruniyon ke saath mein,
Bade chaav se langdi khel rahi thi!
Kyonki, main hoon pachpan se pare, mann hai bachpan ka.
Khil-khilahat aankhen hain utsaah bhari.
Do buzurg mujh pe chillane lage,
"Are sharm kar, tere baal safed ho chale, magar akkal nahin aayi?
Do choti karke, chhote bachchon jaise kapde pehen lene se,
jawani wapas nahin aa jaati, girogi to haddiyaan toot jaayengi."
Maine apna khelna roka nahin.
Magar ghar aane ke baad, raat ko bistar mein pade-pade yeh vichaar aaya –
Umr meri kuch bhi ho, kya main nirjeev hone se pehle hi meri urja ko mukt kar doon apne mann se,
Aur sthagit kar doon apni kanchan kaaya?
Agale din phir woh do buzurg mile, aur wahi rok-tok ka aalaap.
Maine palat ke kaha,
"Chachaji, aap apni zindagi barson mein ginte raho,
Main to sundar yaadein sametne mein maanti hoon.
Aap samay ki sooiyaan batoro,
Main to harsh-ullaas ke khule vichaaron ko lekar,
Beh chali aashaaon ki nadi mein,
Jis mein aaya hai sailaab!"

# सौंदर्या

नमस्ते, मैं हूँ सौंदर्या, उर्फ खुबसूरती!
भोर का सूरज है मेरी बींदी ।
सुबह की ओसबिन्दू की मोतियों की लडी में पिरोया सुरजमुखी,
मेरा माँगटिका ।
आभा पर लेहराती लालिमा मेरी चुनर,
हवाओं ने बुना वसंत के फूलों से मेरा
सतरंगी घाघरा, ये है, हवाओं का असीम हुनर
सदा बहार कलियाँ, मेरी लहरों जैसी जुलफों
में बस्ती, ताकी उनका रंग ना कभी पड़े फिका।
द्वादशी का चांद मेरी बालियाँ...
टिम-टिमाती, छोटे से जुगनु मेरे नारंगी चूड़ियां...
कल-कल बेहती छोटी सी नेहर मेरे घूंघरू...
छम-छम बजती जाये, जब मैं बेहते पानी के
पथरों पे से, कूदती हुई गुज़रूँ।
धरा की लाल मिट्टी मेरे पैरों का अलता...
निशित का निमीर मेरी आँखों में काजल सा पिघलता
फूलों-पत्तों से लदी लताए मेरी पैंजनी।
माँ प्रकृती ने है मुझे जना।
इसी लिए मैंने श्रृंगार को सजना सिखाया,
क्यों कि मैं हूँ सौंदर्या।

# Saundarya

Namaste, main hoon Saundarya, urf khoobsurti!
Bhor ka sooraj hai meri bindi.
Subah ki osbindu ki motiyon ki ladi mein piroya surajmukhi,
mera maang-tika.
Aabha par lehrati laalima meri chunar,
Hawaaon ne buna vasant ke phoolon se mera
Satrangi ghaaghra, yeh hai hawaaon ka aseem hunar.
Sada bahaar kaliyaan, meri lehron jaisi zulfon
Mein basti, taaki unka rang na kabhi pade pheeka.
Dwaadashi ka chaand meri baaliyaan...
Tim-timaati, chhote se jugnu meri naarangi choodiyaan...
Kal-kal behti chhoti si nehar mere ghunghroo...
Chham-chham bajti jaaye, jab main behte paani ke
Pathron pe se, koodti hui guzroon.
Dhara ki laal mitti mere pairon ka alta...
Nishit ka nimeer meri aankhon mein kaajal sa pighalta.
Phoolon-patton se ladi lataayein meri painjani.
Maa Prakriti ne hai mujhe jana.
Isi liye maine shringaar ko sajna sikhaaya,
Kyonki main hoon Saundarya.

# दरमियाँ

रात की सियाही घटने के बाद
और सुबह की पहली किरण से पहले,
टिम-टिमाते तारों के ओजल होने के बाद
और धूप, धरा पर बिखरने से पहले,
इन दोनों घडियों के बीच में,
आकाश पर जो फैलती है गुलाबी गुलाल की आभा,
इस अंतराल को भोर कहते हैं सभी।
इन दोनों के दरमियां सदियों का साथ है
फिर भी क्षण भर का साथ नहीं !
तरुण तीस के सपनों के योवन की वसंत ऋतू
और नब्बे की थमती, ठिठुरती उम्र की शीत काल के बीच में
साठ की उम्र ना भरी जवानी, ना खडकता बुडापा,
बल्कि हकीकत की मानो तपती ग्रीष्म ऋतू|
मानो ज़िम्मेदारी और फर्ज के क़र्ज़ से,
सब करने की आवश्यकता और कुछ भी न कर ने
की परिस्थिति के दरमियां हिचकोले खाती है।
खुद की इच्छाएँ , महत्वाकांक्षाएं ,
और क्षमताएं जीवन की झुलसती
रेत में, हम जिंदा दफनाते है।
अक्सर बच्चों के उजले भविष्य की नैया, समय के सागर पर अपने प्यार
और हिम्मत की पतवार से पार लगाते हैं।
इस आने वाले कल और बीते हुए कल की जद्द-ओ-जहद के दर्मीयाँ
अपने आज की आहुती क्यों चढ़ाते हैं?
हर हिचकिचाती 'हाँ' और नागवारा 'ना' के बीच एक गहरी सोच में डूबा
'शायद' होता है।
चहकती चुप्पी और चीखते संन्नाटों के दर्मीयाँ
एक गूंजती खामोशी होती हैं।

शब्दों के बैमाने अर्थों और अधूरे जज़्बातों के वाक्यों के बीच में एक
असीम अकेलापन होता है।
रोते बिलखते इस संसार ने ली पहली साँस और आखरी...
मुक्ती की मरहमी, सफ़ेद कफ़न में।
इन दोनों के दुर्मीयाँ एक खिलखिलाती सौगात होती है।
इसी का नाम, जिंदगी है।

# Darmiyaan

Raat ki siyaahi ghatne ke baad
Aur subah ki pehli kiran se pehle,
Tim-timaate taaron ke ojhal hone ke baad
Aur dhoop, dhara par bikharne se pehle,
In dono ghadiyon ke beech mein,
Aakaash par jo phailti hai gulaabi gulaal ki aabha,
Is antaraal ko bhor kehte hain sabhi.
In dono ke darmiyaan sadiyon ka saath hai,
Phir bhi kshan bhar ka saath nahin!
Tarun tees ke sapnon ke yauvan ki vasant ritu
Aur nabbe ki thamti, thithurti umr ki sheet kaal ke beech mein,
Saath ki umr na bhari jawaani, na khadakta budhaapa,
Balki haqeeqat ki maano tapti greeshm ritu.
Maano zimmedaari aur farz ke qarz se,
Sab karne ki aavashyakta aur kuch bhi na karne
Ki paristhiti ke darmiyaan hichkole khaati hai.
Khud ki ichchhaen, mahatvaakaankshaen aur kshamataen
Jeevan ki jhulsati ret mein, hum zinda dafnaate hain.
Aksar bachchon ke ujle bhavishya ki naiya,
Samay ke saagar par apne pyaar aur himmat ki patvaar se paar lagaate hain.
Is aane wale kal aur beete hue kal ki jadd-o-jahad ke darmiyaan
Apne aaj ki aahuti kyon chadhaate hain?
Har hichkichaati "haan" aur naagavaara "na" ke beech
Ek gehri soch mein dooba "shaayad" hota hai.
Chahakti chuppi aur cheekhte sannaaton ke darmiyaan
Ek goonjti khaamoshi hoti hai.

Shabdon ke baimaane, arthon aur adhoore jazbaaton ke
vaakyonn ke beech mein
Ek aseem akelapan hota hai.
Rote-bilakhte is sansaar ne li pehli saans aur aakhri...
Mukti ki marhami, safed kafan mein.
In dono ke darmiyaan ek khilkhilaati saugaat hoti hai.
Isi ka naam, zindagi hai.

# तुम हो ना

खुद को हम हमेशा हर मेले में अकेला पाते हैं।
एक अजीब सा अकेलापन, एक चहकती चुप्पी छाई रहती है।
फिर अचानक तेरा मुस्कुराता चेहरा,
सैकडों के सैलाब में तैरता, दिखाई देता है।
मानो जैसे मेरी तन्हाई को साहिल मिल गया।
अब मुझे उम्र का अंधेरा क्या रोकेगा,
मेरे पास तेरा रेशमी स्पर्श और तुम हो ना!
किसी अप्रिय घटना, अनुचित माहोल से
झूझती, या कोई दिल दहलाने वाली बात हो,
वहाँ से मैं कमान से निकले तीर
और खोलते लावा की तरह बह निकली।
चारो ओर घुटन उदासी और मौत का तांडव मन्डरा रहा हो;
तब तेरी आगोश की सुकूनी रजाई,
तेरे दाहीने कँधे का मखमली सिरहाना, और तुम हो ना!
जीवन सफर की हर गुलाबी सुबह,
हर सुरमई शाम और हर धूप-छाव में तेरा
अटूट साथ और तुम हो ना!
हर वसंत रंगीन, हर ऋतु सुहानी, हर मोड़,
हर लम्हाँ यादगार क्योंकि तेरा स्थिर हाथ
और तुम हो ना।
तुम हो ना!
तुम हो ना?
तुम हो ना।

# Tum Hona

Khud ko hum hamesha har mele mein akela paate hain.
Ek ajeeb sa akelapan, ek chahakti chuppi chhaai rehti hai.
Phir achaanak tera muskuraata chehra,
Saikadon ke sailaab mein tairta, dikhaai deta hai.
Maano jaise meri tanhaai ko saahil mil gaya.
Ab mujhe umr ka andhera kya rokega,
Mere paas tera reshmi sparsh aur tum ho na!
Kisi apriya ghatna, anuchit maahol se
Jhoojhti, ya koi dil dahlaane wali baat ho,
Wahaan se main kamaan se nikle teer
Aur kholte laava ki tarah beh nikli.
Chaaro or ghutan, udaasi aur maut ka taandav mandra raha ho;
Tab teri aagosh ki sukooni rajaai,
Tere daahine kandhe ka makhmali sirhaana, aur tum ho na!
Jeevan safar ki har gulaabi subah,
Har surmai shaam aur har dhoop-chhaav mein tera
Atoot saath aur tum ho na!
Har vasant rangeen, har ritu suhaani, har mod,
Har lamha yaadgaar kyonki tera sthir haath
Aur tum ho na.
Tum ho na!
Tum ho na?
Tum ho na.

# क्या आस्माँ सिकुडा गया ?

एक बीज मिट्टी में पनपता है अपनी धरती माँ
की नरम गरम और मर्म गोद में।
एक शिशु कभी करवट लेता, कमी हाथ पैर मारता, या सिमट कर,
सो जाता अपनी माँ की कोख में।
माँ मुस्कुराती ये सोच कर मेरा बच्चा जिंदा है!
इस नन्ही सी जान के जन्म से पहले ही परिवार वाले,
जन्म के बाद स्कूल, कक्षा, कालेज, दफतर, दोस्त और फिर जीवनसाथी ये
सब समाजवाले अपनी-अपनी, अपेक्षाएँ, महत्वकांक्षाओं, इच्छाओं और
ओधों के बल-बूते पर, रख देते हैं उपनी उम्मीदों और शर्तों की टोकरथा,
इस एक जान के सर पर रख देते है
अपने मजबूत कंधे और कमर तो कस लेता है इंसान,
मगर उसके निजी सपनों की आहुती नहीं सहन कर पाता इंसान|
तो क्या हुआ अगर परिस्तिथी, लोग और माहोल - विश्यला, विपरीत और
विनाशी है तो?
जिंदगी अती सुंदर, सुहानी और अमूल्य है ना?
उसे सम्पूर्णतह अनुबभ करो तो सही!
उसके हर उतार-चढ़ाव धूप-छाँव,
खट्टे-मीठे स्वाद का मज़ा चखो तो सही!
जीवन का जा़यका ऐसा सर चढ़के बोलेगा।
की किसी और हल्के नशे का रंग ना टिकेगा और चड़ेगा ही नहीं।
हम क्या इतने गरीब हो गये कि किसी के लिए
दो अच्छे विचार नहीं, चार मरहमी बोल नहीं,
एक धड़कता दिल नहीं??
इंसानियत का आस्मां इत्ना सिकुड गया,
कि परिंदे मुश्किल से पंख फड़-फड़ा रहे हैं,
और धरती पर इंसान लड़खड़ाकर अकेला दम तोड़ रहा है?

# Kya Aasmaan Sikud Gaya?

Ek beej mitti mein panapta hai apni dharti maa
ki naram-garam aur marm god mein.
Ek shishu kabhi karvat leta, kabhi haath-pair maarta, ya simat kar,
so jaata apni maa ki kokh mein.
Maa muskuraati yeh soch kar, mera bachcha zinda hai!
Is nanhi si jaan ke janm se pehle hi parivaar wale,
janm ke baad school, kaksha, college, daftar, dost aur phir jeevansaathi–
yeh sab samaajwale apni-apni apekshaen, mahatvaakaankshaen,
ichchhaen aur odhon ke bal-boote par,
rakh dete hain apni ummeedon aur sharton ki tokri,
is ek jaan ke sar par rakh dete hain.
Apne majboot kandhe aur kamar to kas leta hai insaan,
magar uske niji sapnon ki aahuti nahin sahan kar paata insaan.
To kya hua agar paristhiti, log aur maahol–
vishaila, vipreet aur vinaashi hai to?
Zindagi ati sundar, suhaani aur amoolya hai na?
Use sampoornatah anubhav karo to sahi!
Uske har utaar-chadhaav, dhoop-chhaanv,
khatte-meethe swaad ka maza chakho to sahi!
Jeevan ka zaayka aisa sar chadh ke bolega,
ki kisi aur halke nashe ka rang na tikega aur chadhega hi nahin.

Hum kya itne gareeb ho gaye ki kisi ke liye
do achche vichaar nahin, chaar marhami bol nahin,
ek dhadakta dil nahin??
Insaaniyat ka aasmaan itna sikud gaya,
ki parinde mushkil se pankh fad-fada rahe hain,
aur dharti par insaan ladkhadaakar akela dum tod raha hai?

# सिसकते सन्नाटे

चंद छन्द, कुछ पंक्तियाँ, थोड़ी कहानियाँ
और अनेक निबंध-लेख सब उमस होते देखा
उबलती, दाल, कडी और सब्ज़ी,
भूनते भुट्टे के साथ बाफ होते देखा।
दराज़ साफ करते एक छोटी सी डिब्बी में मिला
बरसों पहले खोया हुआ मिसराफ
इक पल में मेरे मनमें सोते सितार के सब तार छोड़ गया ।
जैसे कोई स्थीर, शान्त, तालाब के आईने पर,
एक पत्थर फेंक कर उस तालाब के चेहरे पर
ढेर सारी सिलवटे छेड़ गया।
एक रेशम की जामुनी रंग की थैली में एक काँच के तरकश में मीली कुछ
नई-पुरानी तुलिकाएँ
उसी क्षण मस्तिष्क के परदे पर कई अनोखे,
मगर अधुरे चित्रों का मेला सा लग गया
घर-ग्रहस्ती की चक्की में पिस्ती रही।
कलात्मक क्षमताओं को बेबस आँखों से देखती रही।
कभी बेटी, कभी बीवी की देहलीज़ ने रोका,
कभी ममता की चौखट पर बैठी रही।
अनगिन्त मरे हुए सपनों की शवतिर्थ से उठता हुआ धुवाँ,
यादों की गहरी खाई में गुन्जता घना संन्नाटा।
क्योंकि, जब सपने मरते है तो कोई कोलाहल या शोर नहीं होता।
बस अंतर-आत्मा में धीरे-धीरे सुलगते है कुछ दफनाएं अरमान।
और खुले आसमान पर बिखर जाता है
निशब्द कोलाहल,
माना जैसे कोई चद्दर हो सिसकते सन्नाटों की।

# Sisakte Sannate

Chand chhand, kuch panktiyaan, thodi kahaaniyaan
Aur anek nibandh-lekh sab umas hote dekha.
Ubalti daal, kadhi aur sabzi,
Bhoonte bhutte ke saath baaf hote dekha.
Daraaz saaf karte ek chhoti si dibbi mein mila
Barson pehle khoya hua misraaf,
Ik pal mein mere mann mein sote sitaar ke
Sab taar chhod gaya.
Jaise koi sthir, shaant, taalaab ke aaine par,
Ek patthar phenk kar us taalaab ke chehre par
Dher saari silwatein chhed gaya.
Ek resham ki jaamuni rang ki thaili mein,
Ek kaanch ke tarkash mein mili
Kuch nayi-puraani tulikaen,
Usi kshan mastishk ke parde par kai anokhe,
Magar adhoore chitron ka mela sa lag gaya.
Ghar-grahasti ki chakki mein pisti rahi.
Kalaatmak kshamtaaon ko bebas aankhon se dekhti rahi.
Kabhi beti, kabhi beevi ki dehleez ne roka,
Kabhi mamta ki chaukhat par baithi rahi.
Anginat mare hue sapnon ki shavteerth se uthta hua dhuaan,
Yaadon ki gehri khaai mein goonjta ghana sannata.
Kyonki, jab sapne marte hain to koi kolaahal ya shor nahin hota.
Bas antar-aatma mein dheere-dheere sulagte hain kuch dafnaaye armaan.
Aur khule aasmaan par bikhar jaata hai
Nishabd kolaahal,
Maano jaise koi chaddar ho sisakte sannaaton ki.

# मुसाफिर हूँ यारों

इस दुनियाँ में मेरी दुनियाँ ढूंढने निकली हूँ।
मैं तो हकिकत से परे सपनों की दुनियाँ की मुसाफिर हूँ।
सितार के तारों की झन्कार में मेरे दिल की तेज़ धड़कन छलके ।
पुराने गीतों में मुझे दिखे आपने अतित के दोस्तों की झलकें।
हाथ पकड़ कर तुलिका ऐसी चली जैसे कोई प्यारी सहेली
कागज़ पे खिलती आकृतियाँ दर्शाएं जीवन की अनगिनत पहेली।
काल्पनिक कहानियाँ और कविताओं ने शब्दों का जाल बिखेरा
एक ऐसा जहान, जहाँ पर धन सिर्फ सिक्कें नहीं,
मगर मन की भावनाओं का मूल हो ।
सुर, साज़ और सोज़ से भरी सच्चाई, खुली किताब सा व्यक्तित्व ।
क्या ऐसा ठिकाना है कहीं,
क्या ऐसे माहोल का है अस्तित्व ?
ऐ पटरी तू जो वास्तविकता के शहर से,
गुज़रती है क्या तेरी भी मंज़िल है सपनो का शिखर?
तो, अपनी राह एक है।
मुझे भी ले चल अपने संग उस मुकाम पर!

# Musaafir Hu Yaaro

Is duniya mein meri duniya dhoondhne nikli hoon.
Main to haqeeqat se pare sapnon ki duniya ki musaafir hoon.
Sitaar ke taaron ki jhankaar mein mere dil ki tez dhadkan chhalke.
Puraane geeton mein mujhe dikhen apne ateet ke doston ki jhalkein.
Haath pakad kar tulika aisi chali jaise koi pyaari saheli,
Kaagaz pe khilti aakritiyaan darshaayen jeevan ki anginat paheli.
Kaalpanik kahaaniyaan aur kavitaon ne shabdon ka jaal bikhera,
Ek aisa jahaan, jahan par dhan sirf sikkein nahin,
Magar mann ki bhaavnaaon ka mool ho.
Sur, saaz aur soz se bhari sachchaai,
Khuli kitaab sa vyaktitva.
Kya aisa thikaana hai kahin,
Kya aise maahol ka hai astitva?
Ai patri, tu jo vaastavikta ke shehar se guzarti hai,
Kya teri bhi manzil hai sapnon ka shikhar?
To, apni raah ek hai.
Mujhe bhi le chal apne sang us mukaam par!

# कुम्भार

मिट्टी, जिससे हम निकले हैं, उसी में मिट जाएंगे।
कुम्भार, जो कलाकार और कारिगर, दोनो है,
गडता आकृतीयाँ अलग-अलग है !
सुन्दर, सुडोल, सटीक और सुमधुर...
हमारा अदृश्य सृजनहार गडता हमे माटी के पुतलो सा।
फूंक देता हम में साँसे और रंग देता
हज़ारों ख़्वाहिशें, जज़्बातों और जबानों से।
रोज नया खेल हम रचते, हँसते, बोलते लड़ते-जगडते,
फिर से मिल जाते !
कब आए, कब चले गये,
मिट्टी से निकले थे, मिट्टी में समा गए!।

# Kumbhaar

Mitti, jisse hum nikle hain, usi mein mit jaayenge.
Kumbhaar, jo kalaakar aur kaarigar, dono hai,
Gadhta aakritiyaan alag-alag hai!
Sundar, sudol, sateek aur sumadhur...
Hamaara adrishya srijanhaar gadhta humein maati ke putlon sa.
Phoonk deta hum mein saansein aur rang deta
Hazaaron khwaahishen, jazbaaton aur jabaanon se.
Roz naya khel hum rachhte, hanste, bolte, ladte-jhagadte,
Phir se mil jaate!
Kab aaye, kab chale gaye,
Mitti se nikle the, mitti mein sama gaye!

# कल, आज और कल

समय का पहिया जीवन की पगडण्डी पर
घूमता चला जा रहा है।
बीते हुए कल की डगर से,
आज की हकीकत की गलियों से गुज़रता
एक उज्जवल भविष्य के रास्ते पर चले-चला है।
कितने वादे टूटे, कौन करीबी ने खंजर भोंका पीठ में, कहाँ रह गए
सुन्दर सपने बीते बरसों के?
बेतुके सवाल और विरोधाभाशी ज़वाबों से
आज की परिस्तिथी पर कोई प्रभाव नहीं पड़ेगा।
क्योंकि आज, संसारिक, व्यवहारिक, नैतिक और
दैनिक जिम्मेदारियों की गाड़ी खींचनी पड़ेगी;
पहिए टूट जाएंगे रिश्तों के।
चल उठ दिल-ए-नादान,
इस इतीहास को लगातार फिर से दोहराते समय के शिकंजे
से तुझे निकलना पड़ेगा।
एक सोचे-समझे, सकारात्मक, मज़बूत, सुन्दर, आने वाले कल का निर्माण
कर ।
बीत गया जो, समय वो था- आज तेरे सामने है।
आने वाले, चमकते कल का सृजन कर।

## Kal, Aaj aur Kal

Samay ka pahiya jeevan ki pagdandi par
Ghoomta chala ja raha hai.
Beete hue kal ki dagar se,
Aaj ki haqeeqat ki galiyon se guzarta,
Ek ujjwal bhavishya ke raaste par chale-chala hai.
Kitne vaade toote, kaun kareebi ne khanjar bhonka peeth mein,
Kahan reh gaye sundar sapne beete barson ke?
Betuke sawaal aur virodhaabhaashi jawaabon se
Aaj ki paristhiti par koi prabhaav nahin padega.
Kyonki aaj, sansaarik, vyavahaarik, naitik aur
Dainik zimmedaariyon ki gaadi kheenchni padegi;
Pahiye toot jaayenge rishton ke.
Chal uth dil-e-naadaan,
Is itihaas ko lagaataar phir se dohraate
Samay ke shikanje se tujhe nikalna padega.
Ek soche-samjhe, sakaaraatmak, mazboot, sundar,
Aane wale kal ka nirmaan kar.
Beet gaya jo, samay woh tha—
Aaj tere saamne hai.
Aane wale, chamakte kal ka srijan kar.

# करलो ना दोस्ती !

करलो ना दोस्ती इन हवाओं से,
वो ताकत बन कर पंख देंगी आपके लक्ष्य को।
करलो न दोस्ती इस पथरीली पथ से उसका उबड़–खाबड़ रास्ता लिपटती
धुंधू में जो खोये जा रहा है आपके इरादे मज़बूत और सफर को थोड़े
आसान कर देगा |
करलो ना दोस्ती इन घटाओं से,
उनके लाखों बूंदों के जालनरंग के ताल पे तुम भी नाच लो ना |
जैसे ये पंछी, विशाल वसुंधरा और
पंच भूत आनंद तांडव कर रहे हैं,
वैसे तुम भी कौंधती बिजली से  ताल मिलालो ना।
करलो ना दोस्ती  उमंग की उठती लेहरों से, हर चट्टान छोटी लगेगी...
जैसे लेहरें संगेमरमर और शिलाजित के टीलों के टकराकर नई लहरें
करलो ना दोस्ती इन बहारों, ग्रीष्म शरद और हर ऋतु से |
समय के घूमते पहिए ओर बदलते रिश्तों से।
करलो ना दोस्ती सच्चे दिल के रिश्तों से ।
मिटा दोना ये 'मैं' और 'तुम' के फासले, एक निखालस 'हम' से।

# Karlo na dosti!

Karlo na dosti in hawaaon se,
Woh taakat ban kar pankh dengi aapke lakshya ko.
Karlo na dosti is pathreeli path se,
Uska ubad-khaabad raasta lipat-ti dhundh mein jo
Khoye ja raha hai, aapke iraade mazboot
Aur safar ko thoda aasaan kar dega.
Karlo na dosti in ghataaon se,
Unki laakhon boondon ke jalnaranag ke taal pe
Tum bhi naach lo na.
Jaise yeh panchhi, vishaal vasundhara aur panch bhoot
Aanand taandav kar rahe hain,
Vaise tum bhi kaundhti bijli se
Taal mila lo na.
Karlo na dosti umang ki uthti lehron se,
Har chattan chhoti lagegi...
Jaise lehrain sangemarmar aur shilajit ke teelon se
Takraakar nayi lehrain ban jaati hain.
Karlo na dosti in bahaaron, greeshm, sharad
Aur har ritu se.
Samay ke ghoomte pahiye aur badalte rishton se.
Karlo na dosti sachche dil ke rishton se.
Mita do na yeh 'main' aur 'tum' ke faasle,
Ek nikhaalas 'hum' se.

# रात

रात है कुदरत का काजल,
जो होले-होले दिन की आँखों की बिछे जाता है।
ताकी सम्पूर्ण मानवता सपनो का बिछोना
ओढ़कर कल के सुन्दर लक्षय को प्राप्त कर सके।
आज की सारी अच्छी-बुरी घटनाएँ ,
फतेह–शिकस्तें, आधी-पूरी ख्वाहिशें,
सब हकिकतों की पलके मूंदकर लोग सो जाते हैं।
यह रात तो हताश ज़िंदगी की वो काली सुरंग है जो कल की नयी,
उमंगभरी, आशाओं से चनककती उजली
सुबह की तरफ जाती है ।

# Raat

Raat hai kudrat ka kaajal,
jo hole-hole din ki aankhon par bichh jaata hai.
Taaki sampoorn maanavta sapnon ka bichhona
odhkarr kal ke sundar lakshya ko praapt kar sake.
Aaj ki saari achhi-buri ghatnaayein, fateh-shekasten,
aadhi-poori khwaahishen,
sab haqeeqaton ki palken mudkar log so jaate hain.
Yah raat to hataash zindagi ki vo kaali surang hai
jo kal ki nayee,
umang-bhari, aashaon se chanakti ujli
subah ki taraf jaati hai.

# मैं शून्य हूँ

हाँ मैं वो शून्य हूँ
जो क्षण भर में एक लाख
को एक करोड़ कर दे।
निशित का मैं वो तिमीर हूँ जो आने वाली सुबह की
उषा किरण को शुभ सर्जाए।
मेहनत में, मैं, पसीने का मोती हूँ जो गुमनामी के अंधकार में लुप्त हो गया!
मगर जिसने प्रशंसा और बढ़ावा देखा,
वो आनंद तान्डव के नशे में मगन हो गया
रंगों में, मैं, वो श्वेत हूँ, जो प्रकृती के हर रंग को ज्यादा निखारू!
फिर वो खुन्सी लालिमा हो, आकाश का निलाम्बरी हो, सूर्य का पिताम्बरी
था, वसुन्धरा की हरियाली – मैं इन्हे उभारू।
मैं गगन का वो अंधकर हूँ, जिस के कारण,
नज़रे खिले चांद को निहारे।
मानवी जीव के मन की घुटन में
मैं उनके साथ घुटती हूँ।
ताकी वो खुल्ली श्वास की सुधा पा सके।
जीवन के दुखों का मैं वो अश्रू बिन्दु हूँ,
जो हर्ष से भरी स्मीत का सच्चा मोल कराए।
जीस्से दूसरों का खिलता और चमकता व्यक्तित्व
सृष्टि में, मैं, वो निराकार, निरंतर अस्तित्व हूँ
मेरी अर्थि से पहले मेरी अस्ति, और
उस से भी पहले, मेरी हस्ती मिटाने से,
मेरा अस्तित्व नहीं मिट जाएगा!
मुझे अपनाओ या नहीं,
मुझे चाहे तुच्छ या विराट कहो,
मुझे मानो था अमान्य करार दो,
मगर मुझे नकार तो नहीं सकोगे !
हाँ मैं शून्य हूँ, मगर सुषुप्त या सुन्न नहीं हूँ!

# Main Shunya Hoon

Haan main woh shoonya hoon
Jo kshan bhar mein ek laakh
Ko ek crore kar de.
Nishit ka main woh timeer hoon jo aane wali subah ki usha kiran ko shubh sarjaaye.
Mehnat mein, main, paseene ka moti hoon jo gumnaami ke andhkaar mein lupt ho gaya!
Magar jisne prashansa aur badhaava dekha,
Woh aanand taandav ke nashe mein magan ho gaya.
Rangon mein, main, woh shvet hoon, jo prakriti ke har rang ko zyaada nikhaaru!
Phir woh khunsi laalima ho, aakaash ka neelaambari ho, soorya ka pitaambari ho, vasundhara ki hariyaali - main inhein ubhaaru.
Main gagan ka woh andhkar hoon, jiske kaaran,
Nazrein khile chaand ko nihaarein.
Maanavi jeev ke mann ki ghutan mein
Main unke saath ghut-ti hoon,
Taaki woh khulli shwaas ki sudha paa saken.
Jeevan ke dukhon ka main woh ashru bindu hoon,
Jo harsh se bhari smeet ka sachcha mol karaaye.
Jisse doosron ka khilta aur chamakta vyaktitva...
Srishti mein, main, woh niraakaar, nirantar astitva hoon.
Meri arthii se pehle meri asti,
Aur us se bhi pehle, meri hasti mitaane se,
Mera astitva nahin mit jaayega!
Mujhe apnaao ya nahin,

Mujhe chaahe tuchchh ya viraat kaho,
Mujhe maano ya amaanya karaar do,
Magar mujhe nakaaar to nahin sakoge!
Haan, main shoonya hoon,
Magar sushupt ya sunn nahin hoon!

# मैं तो सिर्फ एक आइना हूँ

जब कुछ चेहरे मन्द-मन्द मुस्कुराते
तिरछी नज़र के इशारे करते देखता हूँ...
जब प्यार कि धरती पर विश्वास की बगिया खिलते देखता हूँ...
तो मैं भी मुस्कुरा देता हूँ।
जो देखता हूँ, वही दिखाता हूँ,
मैं तो सिर्फ एक आईना हूँ।
जब कायदा- कानून का किला बिखर जाये,
दंगे-फसाद बढे, मकान, पुल,
उद्योग और घर टूटे;
देशों में अमन टूटे, किसी का दिल या रिश्तें टूटे,
तो मेरे भी मस्तिष्क पर और चार सिलवटें गहरी हो जाती हैं।
मेरे भी चेहरे पर विश्वासघात, षडयंत्र और दुश्मनी का कीचड
आँसु बन कर बेहता है।
जो देखता हूँ, वही दिखाता हूँ।
आखिर, मैं तो सिर्फ एक आईना हूँ।
कूटनीती के खन्जर से, इन्सानियत के कैनवास पर, किसी की भावनाओं
का खुरदरा चेहरा देखकर डर जाते हो ?
दोस्त, यही तो हकीकत है।
हकीकत तो दो धारी तलवार है।
ढंगसे चलाओ तो रक्षक वरना भक्षक ।
ये दो धारी तलवार तो, नंगी, निष्ठुर और निस्पक्ष है।
डरो मत, कुछ करो, इस भयानक चेहरे को
मृदु, सुहाना और सुन्दर बनाओ।
मुझे तोडने से क्या फायदा है?
जो देखता हूँ वही दिखाता हूँ।
मैं तो सिर्फ एक आईना हूँ।

# Main To Sirf Ek Aaina Hoon

Jab kuch chehre mand-mand muskuraate,
Tirchhi nazar ke ishaare karte dekhta hoon...
Jab pyaar ki dharti par vishvaas ki bagiya khilte dekhta hoon...
To main bhi muskura deta hoon.
Jo dekhta hoon, wahi dikhaata hoon,
Main to sirf ek aaina hoon.
Jab kaayda-kaanoon ka kila bikhar jaaye,
Dange-fasaad badhein, makaan, pul,
Udyog aur ghar toote;
Deshon mein aman toote, kisi ka dil ya rishte toote,
To mere bhi mastishk par aur chaar silwatein gehri ho jaati hain.
Mere bhi chehre par vishvaasghaath, shadayantra
Aur dushmani ka keechad aansu ban kar behta hai.
Jo dekhta hoon, wahi dikhaata hoon.
Aakhir, main to sirf ek aaina hoon.
Kootneeti ke khanjar se, insaaniyat ke canvas par,
Kisi ki bhaavnaaon ka khurdura chehra dekhkar dar jaate ho?
Dost, yahi to haqeeqat hai.
Haqeeqat to do dhaari talwaar hai.
Dhang se chalaao to rakshak, varna bhakshak.
Yeh do dhaari talwaar to, nangi, nishthur aur nispaksh hai.
Daro mat, kuch karo, is bhayaanak chehre ko
Mridu, suhaana aur sundar banaao.
Mujhe todne se kya faayda hai?
Jo dekhta hoon, wahi dikhaata hoon.
Main to sirf ek aaina hoon.

# कौन - Who?

हाँ सब चेहरे पहचाने से लगते हैं।
हाँ, सब के नाम के साथ कोई न कोई रिश्ता है।
मगर गुमनामी की खाई से उभारे,
दौड़ते विचारों के चीखते संन्नाटों को सुने,
और मन की बोलती खामोशी को चुने,
एसा कोई अपना सा गैर या गैरों में अपना कोई नहीं
हकीकत में हर कोई अपनी राह और रुकावटों से खुद ही सूझता है।
मगर दिल है कि दूसरों में वह करीब सा ढूंढ़ता है,
वास्तव में नहीं तो सपनो में सही।
हर किसी को हाथ ऊँचा करके,
अपनी बात स्थापित करना तो आता है
मगर किसी का हाथ थामकर,
निस्वार्थ होकर संग चलना, ये पता ही नहीं।
अगर सब मेरे, सब अपने चहितों की भीड हो,
तो बेगाने, पराए, अनजाने कितने,
कौन और कहाँ होंगे?

# Kaun - Who?

Haan sab chehre pehchaane se lagte hain.
Haan, sab ke naam ke saath koi na koi rishta hai.
Magar gumnaami ki khaai se ubhaare,
Daudte vichaaron ke cheekhte sannaaton ko sune,
Aur mann ki bolti khaamoshi ko chune,
Aisa koi apna sa gair ya gairon mein apna koi nahin.
Haqeeqat mein har koi apni raah aur rukaavaton se khud hi soojhta hai.
Magar dil hai ki doosron mein woh qareeb sa dhoondhta hai,
Vaastav mein nahin to sapnon mein sahi.
Har kisi ko haath ooncha karke,
Apni baat sthaapit karna to aata hai,
Magar kisi ka haath thaamkar,
Nisvaarth hokar sang chalna, yeh pata hi nahin.
Agar sab mere, sab apne chahiton ki bheed ho,
To begaane, paraaye, anjaane kitne,
Kaun aur kahaan honge?

# मृगि तृष्णा!

सावन की एक सुरमई शाम को,
अपनी छत पर लेटे लेटे
छटते घने  बादलों के बीच से पिघलें
सोने सी किरणों को देखते-देखते
घरोंदों को लौटते पंछियों के साथ एक ख़याल आ बैठा,
मेरे बगल में होले-होले।
क्या जन्म लेना, पढ़ना, काम करना,
गृहस्थी संभालना और फिर बिमारी और
बुढ़ापे के थपेड़े खाते मर जाना धीरे-धीरे,
यही है क्या संसार, क्या इसी का नाम जिंदगी है?
सपने पिरोना, कलात्मक बुद्धियों को संजोना कतरा कतरा,
दुनियाँ में साधारण से परे हटकर, कुछ अलग,
अद्भुत स्थापित  करना चुपके-चुपके।
ये सब कुछ मायने नहीं रखता, बताओ ना सच्ची सच्ची?
हकीकत के रेगिस्तान से गुज़रती सड़क पर आगे बड़ते कदमों पर छाले
पड गये चलते-चलते।
मगर मेरा आशावादी मन सपनो की मृगतृष्णा की ओर आत्मविश्वास से
खींचे जाता, बगैर पलक झपकाते ।

# Mrig Trishna!

Saavan ki ek surmai shaam ko,
Apni chhat par lete-lete
Chhatte ghane baadalon ke beech se pighlein
Sone si kiranon ko dekhte-dekhte,
Gharondon ko lautte panchhiyon ke saath ek khayaal aa baitha,
Mere bagal mein hole-hole.
Kya janm lena, padhna, kaam karna,
Grihasthi sambhaalna aur phir bimaari aur
Budhaape ke thapede khaate mar jaana dheere-dheere,
Yahi hai kya sansaar, kya isi ka naam zindagi hai?
Sapne piroona, kalaatmak buddhiyon ko sanjona katra-katra,
Duniya mein saadhaaran se pare hatkar, kuch alag,
Adbhut sthaapit karna chupke-chupke.
Yeh sab kuch maayne nahin rakhta, batao na sachchi-sachchi?
Haqeeqat ke registaan se guzarti sadak par
Aage badhte kadmon par chhaale pad gaye chalte-chalte.
Magar mera aashaavaadi mann sapnon ki mriga-trishna ki or
Aatmavishvaas se khinche jaata, bagair palak jhapkaate.

# रात रानी

पिघलते मक्खन के जैसी तेरी खिली कलियों का गुच्छा !
क्यारि-क्यारि रंगबे-रंगी फूल, मगर तेरे जैसा न कोई,
किसी बगियाँ, किसी गुन्चा-गुन्चा।
तेरी मनमोहक सुंगध से मदहोश सारा आलम।
क्या पशु, पक्षी, क्या बच्चा, क्या बूढ़ा या किसी का बालम।
तू जागती सारी रतिया, दुनियाँ अपने वश में कर के गहरी नींद सुलाती
तुझे देख दिल में इंसानियत पर भरोसा
जगता, चाहे कितना ही लोग ठगते या समय रुलाता।
तू सौंदर्य, सुहाने ऐहसास, और दिल को लुभाती तरुनी हैं |
ए रात रानी, तू सबके दिल की रानी है ।

# Raat Raani

Pighalte makkhan ke jaisi teri khili kaliyon ka guchchha!
Kyaari-kyaari rang-be-rangi phool, magar tere jaisa na koi, kisi bagiyaan, kisi guncha-guncha.
Teri manmohak sugandh se madhosh saara aalam.
Kya pashu, pakshi, kya bachcha, kya boodha ya kisi ka baalam.
Tu jaagti saari ratiya, duniya apne vash mein kar ke gehri neend sulaati.
Tujhe dekh dil mein insaaniyat par bharosa
Jaagta, chaahe kitna hi log thagte ya samay rulaata.
Tu saundarya, suhaane ehsaas, aur dil ko lubhaati taruni hai.
Ae raat raani, tu sabke dil ki raani hai.

# नज़म

दिल में जो मूक जज़्बातों की घुटन है, कुछ अन्सुनी बातें, कुछ टूटे वादे हैं,
कुछ आधे जुडे, खुछ खिचे, अलग-थलग कुछ रिश्ते हैं।
कुछ अधूरी ख्वाहिशें, कुछ बिखरे सपने है।
इन सब को कागज़ पे बोलों की लड़ी में पिरोकर उतारो।
इस दबी मान्सिक काई को बाहर उभारों!!
किसी कविता, छन्द, बज़्म, या एक नज़्म में निखारो।

# Nazm

Dil mein jo mook jazbaaton ki ghutan hai, kuchh ansuni baatein, kuchh toote waade hain.
Kuchh aadhe jude, khuchh khiche, alag-thalag kuchh rishte hain.
Kuchh adhoori khwaahishein, kuchh bikhre sapne hain.
In sab ko kaagaz pe bolon ki ladi mein pirokar utaaro.
Is dabi maansik kai ko baahar ubhaaro!!
Kisi kavita, chand, bajm, ya ek nazm mein nikhaaro.

# पतझड़

हर भीड से भरे अन्जानो के मेले में
हर अपने से रिश्तों के सज़ते-बिखरते झमेले में,
हर समय और सोच की करवट में हम सब अकेले है।
हर सपने के टूटने की आहट में,
हर विश्वास के छलावे के अविश्वास में,
हर स्थिर पड़ाव पर जीवन की नैया डोलती है,
उस वक्त में, हर बार
उम्रभर का त्याग एक गलत अन्देशे से हारता है,
एसे समय में, हम सब अकले हैं।
जब पतझड में पत्ते न होने से पेड़ की शाख सूनी लगती है,
मगर जब सावन में भी वो पेड़ फिर से नहीं लहलहाता, और उस पर
बिजली गिरती है,
जब झूठ का नगाडा जोरो शोरों से बजता है,
तब सच्च के सितार की सुमधुर सरगम सुनाई नहीं देती है।
जब सूने दिल के सागर किनारे की लेहरें टकराती है तब नहीं,
जब अपनी हँसी-खुशी मैं अपने आप को भूल जाते हैं, तब भी नहीं।
मगर, जब हर कोई अपनी सुविधा और अनुकूलता अनुसार
आपको याद करता है;
तब हम सही मायने में, निसंदेह, अकेले होते है
आस-पास के लोग छोड़ दे या साथ छूट जाये,
तब मन उदास होता है,
मगर जब खुद की याद भी मीट जाए
तब, हम सच्च में हताश और अकेले होते हैं।

# Patjhad

Har bheed se bhare anjaanon ke mele mein,
Har apnon se rishton ke sajte-bikharte jhamele mein,
Har samay aur soch ki karvat mein hum sab akele hain.
Har sapne ke tootne ki aahat mein,
Har vishvaas ke chhalaave ke avishvaas mein,
Har sthir padaav par jeevan ki naiya dolti hai,
Us waqt mein, har baar,
Umr-bhar ka tyaag ek galat andeshe se haarta hai,
Aise samay mein, hum sab akele hain.
Jab patjhad mein patte na hone se ped ki shaakh sooni lagti hai,
Magar jab saavan mein bhi woh ped phir se nahin lahlahata, aur us par bijli girti hai,
Jab jhooth ka nagaada zoron-shoron se bajta hai,
Tab sach ke sitaar ki sumadhur sargam sunaai nahin deti hai.
Jab soone dil ke saagar kinaare ki lehrain takraati hain tab nahin,
Jab apni hansi-khushi mein apne aap ko bhool jaate hain, tab bhi nahin.
Magar, jab har koi apni suvidha aur anukoolta anusaar aapko yaad karta hai;
Tab hum sahi maaynon mein, nissandeh, akele hote hain.
Aas-paas ke log chhod dein ya saath chhoot jaaye,
Tab mann udaas hota hai,
Magar jab khud ki yaad bhi mit jaaye,
Tab, hum sach mein hataash aur akele hote hain.

# एक मुलाकात अपने आपसे

आज, अभी, अपने आप से मुलाकात हो गई।
जैसे मेरे होने की नदियाँ, मेरे व्यतित्त्व के सागर से मिल गई।
सब एहसासों की गहराई से बस एक ही
मोती उभारा है अपने आप में मैं पर्याप्त हूँ।
मैं खुद का साहिल, मैं खुद ही सूरज-चाँद।
अपने आप में मैं संपूर्ण सृष्टि समाई हुँ।

# Ek Mulakaat Apne Aapse

Aaj, abhi, apne aap se mulaakaat ho gayi.
Jaise mere hone ki nadiyaan, mere vyaktitva ke saagar se mil gayi.
Sab ehsaason ki gehraai se bas ek hi
Moti ubhaara hai – apne aap mein main paryaapt hoon.
Main khud ka saahil, main khud hi sooraj-chaand.
Apne aap mein main sampoorn shrishti samaai hu.

# शहादत

ऐ वतन तुझपे में सो-सो बार वारी जाँऊ।
मेरे घरवालों संग तीज त्यौहार, फिर अगले जन्म में मना लूँगा।
माँ से लोरी, फिर अगले जन्म में सुन लूँगा।
पर ये जनम तो मेरी भारत भूमी की गरिमा और आत्मसम्मान पे न्यौछावर
कर के रहुगा।

# Shahaadat

Ai watan tujhpe main sau-sau baar waari jaan jaaun.
Mere gharwaalon sang teej-tyohaar, phir agle janm mein mana
loonga.
Maa se lori, phir agle janm mein sun loonga.
Par yeh janm to meri Bharat bhoomi ki garima aur
aatmasammaan pe nyauchhaavar kar ke rahunga.

# अगर तुम...

अगर तुम साथ हो तो अंधेरे में भी रास्ते मिल जाते हैं।
प्रेम की बगिया में हमारे विश्वास का गुलाब हमेशा खिला रहेगा,
क्यूँकि हम इस जिवन रथ के समान, अटूट पहिये है।
हम साथ हैं तो पतझड़ में भी खुशी की बगिया खिला लेंगे।

# Agar Tum...

Agar tum saath ho to andhere mein bhi raaste mil jaate hain.
Prem ki bagiya mein humaare vishvaas ka gulaab hamesha khila rahega.
Kyunki hum is jeevan rath ke samaan, atoot pahiye hain.
Hum saath hain to patjhad mein bhi khushi ki bagiya khila lenge.

# संक्रांति

कोई कहे उत्तरायण, कोई लोहरी, और कोई कहे बीहु
और कोई कहे पोंगल या मकर संक्रांति।
चारो ओर अपनी सुन्हरी, घनी चुनरी लेहराते खेत,
ईन्द्रधनुशी फूल,पेड़ो पर लदे फल, मानो निखर उठी हो प्रकृती।
इन त्यौहारों के नाम अनेक मगर ऐहसास अंतर आत्माओ की प्यास,
हर्ष और उल्लास एक नई उपज के साथ, एक नई उम्मीद,
और हौसला जगाता है हर दिल में, जो है पवित्र और नेक ।
हर प्रांत की ज़मीन अपनी हरी-भरी कोख से फ़सल की बौछार रूपी
आर्शिवाद बरसाती है।
उत्तर से दक्षिण, पूरब से पश्चिम,
भारत की हर संस्कृती झूमकर खुशियाँ मनाती है।

# Sankranti

Koi kahe Uttarayan, koi Lohri, aur koi kahe Bihu,
Aur koi kahe Pongal ya Makar Sankranti.
Chaaro or apni sunhari, ghani chunri lehrate khet,
Indradhanushi phool, pedon par lade phal, maano nikhar uthi ho prakriti.
In tyohaaron ke naam anek, magar ehsaas antar-aatmaon ki pyaas,
Harsh aur ullaas ek nayi upaj ke saath, ek nayi umeed,
Aur hausla jagaata hai har dil mein, jo hai pavitra aur nek.
Har praant ki zameen apni hari-bhari kokh se
Fasal ki bauchhaar roopi aashirvaad barsaati hai.
Uttar se dakshin, poorab se pashchim,
Bharat ki har sanskriti jhoomkar khushiyaan manaati hai.

# हमार बतिया सुनो।

कहत रहा ऊ स्विमिंग पूल और दरिया का बड़ा टरकिश तौलिया-
"हम तो सब को लपेट लेते हैं अपनी आगोश में।"
इस पे नाक सिकुड कर वो छोटा 6 by 6 hand napkin बोला -
"हाँ लपेटे में लेते हो।"
गुररा के वो बड़ा टौलिया बोला
"ए, का बोलत रहिन चुटनवा तनिक फिर से तो बताओ।"
कोने में हैंगर पर लटकता Versace का सफेड शर्ट बोला -
"तुम लोग फिर से जगडा शुरू मत करो please
मुझे concentrate करने दो"
"आरे वाह! लाइन पर लटके लटके किस पे लाइन मार रहा है तू जो तेरा
concentration भंग हो रहा है?"
चिड के वो पीली लखनोवी कुर्ती बोली,
चार चांदी के बटन की आंखें फाड के
इतने में तीसरे तार पर दोनों गुलाबी रुमाल एक दूसरे को कोनि मारते हुए
मंद मंद मुस्काए।
केसरी गमच्छा हवा में लहराते हुए बोला -
"आरे उ बिदेशी बाबू - Versa sey- ऊ बेनेटोनवा की आकाशी नीली
लेसवा के घाघरे को ताड रहे हो?"
"Oh shut up you गवार people वो powder blue lace का skirt है,
United Colors of Benetton का!"
यू गुस्से से टोक दिया, पूरी तार पर फैली,
प्राणियों की printwali goan gown!
इस हलचल से धडाम से गिरा tericot pant,
polished marble की जमीन पर!
उसके धक्के से बलखाता इतराता गिरा चिकनकारी पजामा उसी पर!

चौक कर पैंट बोला, "मुझ पर यू गिर रहे हो आदमी हो या पजामा?"
इस पे ऐठ कर पजामा बोला –
"लोजी पैजामें से ही पूछ रहे हो की आदमी हो, या पैजामा, अंधे हो क्या?
दिख नहीं रहा है कि हमऊ ही हैं चिन्ककारी पैजामाँ!"
अचानक सात जोडी मोजों की जूमकर गाने लगी,
"ओजी कोई नहीं, आजाओ कुड़ियां ते मुन्डों,
साडे नाले भाँगडा पाके मौज़ा-ई-मोज़ा कर लो।"
तो उन मोजों के साथ बल्खा के खुशी से, सुन्दर फुलकारी कारीगरीवाले
इंद्रधनुशी रंगीन दुपटे भी गिद्दा पाने लगे।
इनके बाद वाले तार पर सूख रहे थे
कांचिपुरम सिल्क की साडियां और वेश्टि लुंगी
जो इस मेले में हुए जमेले से बहुत ही चिड़े।
साडियों ने कहा, "Oh my God! या कितना डोल नगाडा, अमरा इतना
अच्छा बड़ा बाडर का कलर सभी अमराबाड़ी पे आ गया जी।"
रेशम की वेश्टियां बोल उठी-
"एक तो अम्म extra smooth silk उस पे ये extra sleek steel pipe,
no clip; हम सब half slip! कितना difficulty से लटका है
मालुम है क्या जी?"
इतने कुछ कोलाहल के बाद एक आवाज आई-
"मैंने सब सुन लिया मेरे बच्चों, पर अंत में मैं ही ईजत बचाऊंगा आपकी मैं
हूँ तुम्हारा कच्छा"

दोस्तों, बारिश के मौसम में रात के तीन बजे किचन से पानी पीने के लिए
अपने घर के कॉरिडॉर या पैसेच से गुजरो तो गौर से सुनना अपने आधे
गीले आधे सूखे कपडों को इस लेजे से बतियाते हुए ।
फिर वो जाकिट हो या कुरता पजामा!

# Hamar Batiyaa Suno

Kahat raha oo swimming pool aur dariya ka bada Turkish tauliya -
"Hum to sab ko lapet lete hain apni aagosh mein."
Is pe naak sikud kar woh chhota 6 by 6 hand napkin bola -
"Haan, lapete mein lete ho."
Gurra ke woh bada tauliya bola -
"Ee, ka bolat rahin chutanwa, tanik phir se to bataao."
Kone mein hanger par latakta Versace ka safed shirt bola -
"Tum log phir se jhagda shuru mat karo, please mujhe concentrate karne do."
"Arre wah! Line par latke-latke kis pe line maar raha hai tu, jo tera concentration bhang ho raha hai?"
Chidh ke woh peeli Lakhnavi kurti boli,
Chaar chaandi ke button ki aankhen faad ke.
Itne mein teesre taar par dono gulaabi rumaal
Ek doosre ko koni maarte hue mand-mand muskaaye.
Kesari gamchha hawa mein lehrate hue bola -
"Arre oo bideshi babu - Versa-sey -
oo Benettonwa ki aakaashi neeli lacewa ke ghaaghre ko taad rahe ho?"
"Oh shut up you gawaar people,
woh powder blue lace ka skirt hai,
United Colors of Benetton ka!"
Yoon gusse se tok diya, poori taar par phaili,
praaniyon ki printwali gown ne!
Is halchal se dhadaam se gira tericot pant,
polished marble ki zameen par!
Uske dhakke se balkhaata itraata gira
chikankari pajama usi par!
Chauk kar pant bola -

"Mujh par yoon gir rahe ho, aadmi ho ya pajama?"
Is pe aith kar pajama bola –
"Lo ji, pajame se hi pooch rahe ho ki aadmi ho ya pajama,
andhe ho kya?
Dikh nahin raha ki humau hi hain chikankari pajama!"
Achaanak saat jodi mozon ki jhoom kar gaane lagi –
"O ji koi nahin, aajao kudiyan te mundon,
saade naale bhangda paake mauza-e-moja kar lo."
To un mozon ke saath balkha ke khushi se,
sundar phulkari kaarigari wale indradhanushi rangeen dupatte
bhi gidda paane lage.
Inke baad wale taar par sookh rahi thi
Kanchipuram silk ki saadiyaan aur veshti-lungi,
jo is mele mein hue jhamele se bahut hi chidhe.
Saadiyon ne kaha –
"Oh my God! Yeh kitna dol-nagaada,
amara itna achha bada border ka colour
sabhi amra-baadi pe aa gaya ji."
Resham ki veshtiyan bol uthi –
"Ek to amma extra smooth silk,
us pe yeh extra sleek steel pipe, no clip;
hum sab half slip!
Kitna difficulty se latke hain, maaloom hai kya ji?"
Itne kolahal ke baad ek awaaz aayi –
"Maine sab sun liya mere bachchon,
par ant mein main hi izzat bachaaoonga aapki.
Main hoon tumhara kachcha."
Doston, baarish ke mausam mein raat ke teen baje
kitchen se paani peene ke liye
apne ghar ke corridor ya passage se guzro,
to gaur se sunna
apne aadhe geele, aadhe sookhe kapdon ko
is lehje se batiyaate hue.
Phir woh jacket ho ya kurta-pajama!

# *Poems in Marathi*

# जीवनाची पाठशाला

कोण म्हणतं  की पुस्तक घेऊन वर्गात बसलं तरच शिक्षण पूर्ण होतं?
शिकायची इच्छा असली तर फुल असो की पाखरू, दोघंही रंग-रेखांची
कला शिकवतात
सैनिकासारखी उभी असलेली शिखरमाला ठाम दृढ निश्चय
आणि निडरता शिकवते सतत कलकल वाहणारी नदी,
परिस्थिती कशीही असो, लक्ष्य गाठण्याची प्रेरणा देते.
एकत्र चालणारे रानरेडे हरणे
सहभाग, साथ आणि खऱ्या परिश्रमांची ओळख करून देतात.
लोक कितीही दगड मारोत, काटे टोचोत,
फुल तरीही झाडाकडून शिकतं
कुत्र्याची वफादारी,
कावळ्यांची सामूहिक एकता
मांजराची एकचित्त ध्यान करण्याची क्षमता,
एकत्रित चालणारी, काम करणारी माणसं आपल्याला संघकार्याची ओळख
करून देतात.
सर्व काही शिकवतात.
अनाथ हरणाच्या पिलाला स्वतःच्या दुधाने वाढवणारी हत्तीण
करुणेचा खरा अर्थ समजावते.
ही सगळी अमूल्य मानवी मूल्यं
निसर्गच अनुभवायला देतो.
कोण म्हणतं की पुस्तक घेऊन वर्गात बसलं तरच शिक्षण पूर्ण होतं?
या संघटनामुळे माणुसकी हे सगळं आपल्याला माणुसकीचं वाटतं.

# Jeevan Chi Pathshala

Kon mhant ki pustak gheun vargaat basla tarach shikshan poorn hota?
Shikaaychi ichchha asli tar phool aso ki paakharu,
Doghehi rang-rekhaanchi kala shikavtaat.
Sainikaasaarkhi ubhi asleli shikharmaala
Thaam drudh nishchay
Aani nidarata shikavte.
Satat kal-kal vaahnaari nadi,
Paristhiti kashi hi aso,
Lakshya gaathnyachi prerana dete.
Ektrit chaalnaare raanride harane
Sahbhaag, saath aani kharya parishramanchi olakh karun detaat.
Lok kiti hi dagad maarot, kaate tochot,
Phool tarihi jhaadaakdun shikta.
Kutryaachi vafaadaari,
Kaavlyanchi saamuhik ekta,
Maanjaraachi ekchitt dhyaan karnyachi kshamta,
Ektrit chaalnaari, kaam karnaari maansa
Aaplyala sanghkaaryaachi olakh karun detaat.
Sarv kahi shikavtaat.
Anaath haranaachya pillaala swatachya dudhaane vaadhavnaari haattin
Karunecha khara arth samjaavte.
Hi sagli amoolya maanavi moolya
Nisargach anubhavayla deto.
Kon mhant ki pustak gheun vargaat basla tarach shikshan poorn hota?
Ya sanghatanamule maanuski he sagla aaplyala maanuskech vaatta.

# अहो, या ना की आमच्या चिमणी राणीच्या लग्नात?

आंब्याच्या झाडावरील चिमणा
आणि जांभुळाच्या झाडावरील चिमणी
यांचं आज लग्न आहे.
चार रातरानीच्या स्तंभांच्या मधोमध,
मन मोहक मोगऱ्याची रेशमी दोरीने बांधलेले झुले डोलत होते.
मधोश करणाऱ्या सुगंधी चांदणीचा मांडवा!
उंदीर मामांचा कोल्हापुरी ढोल, वर मंडळी चालली निघत गात,
म्हणत सर्वांना "अहो, या ना की आमच्या चिमणी राणीच्या लग्नात!"

नवधान्यांच्या एकवीस नव्हे पण एकदम एकावन्न पोळी-भाकऱ्या बनवल्या.
पिकलेली केळी, चिकू, पेरू, फणस यांच्या पंधरा चटण्या केल्या.
रवा, दुधी, बीट आणि अननसाचा हलवा पण बनवला.
एवढेच नव्हे ह्यांच्या सोबत आणि शेवटी, सात प्रकारचे पान-विडेही सजून तयार झाले.
अहो, या ना की आमच्या चिमणी राणीच्या लग्नात!

शेजारची पांढरी मांजर आणि तिची चार काळी पिल्लं आली.
ती काळी कुत्री आणि तिची पाच पांढरी पिल्लंदेखील आली.
नदीकाठी राहणारे हत्ती काका–काकू
आणि त्यांच्याबरोबर पंचवीस कुटुंबीय आले.
पलीकडचे–अलिकडचे सगळे प्राणी–पक्षी पण सहभागी झाले.
अहो, तुम्ही पण नक्की या ना,
आमच्या चिमणी राणीच्या लग्नात!

# Aho, ya na ki aamchi Chimni Rani cha lagnaat?

Aambyaachya jhaadaavariil chimna
Aani jaambhulaachya jhaadaavariil chimni
Yaanch aaj lagna aahe.
Chaar raatraaniichya stambhaancha madhomadh,
Man-mohak mogryaachi reshmi doriine baandhleli jhule dolat hoti.
Madhosh karnaarya sugandhi chaandaniicha maandva!
Undeer maamaanchaa Kolhaapuri dhol, var mandali chaarli nighat gaat,
Maltat sarvaanna, "Aho, yaa naa ki aamchyaa chimni raaniichya lagnat!"
Navdhaanyaanchya ekvees navhe pan ekdam ekaavann poli-bhaakryaa banavlya.
Piklele keli, chiku, peru, phanas yaanchyaa pandhra chatnyaa kelyaa.
Ravaa, dudhi, beet aani ananaasaacha halwaa pan banavlaa.
Evdach nave heenchaa shobat aani shevti,
Saat prakaarche paan-bidehi sajun tayaar jhaale.
Aho, yaa naa ki aamchyaa chimni raaniichya lagnat!
Shejaarachi paandhari maanjar aani tichi chaar kaali pillan aali.
Ti kaali kutri aani tichi paach paandhari pillandehi aali.
Nadikathi raahnare haathi kaakaa-kaaku
Aani tyaanchaabarobar panchvees kutumbiya aale.
Palikadche-alikadche sagle praanee-pakshi pal sahabhaagi jhaale.
Aho, tumhi pan nakkich yaa naa,
Aamchyaa chimni raaniichya lagnat!

# ती पण निसर्ग

घराला जर बीज दिलं, तर संपूर्ण वसुंधरेवर
फुलं आणि पानांची चारचौघी पसरते.
स्त्रीला जर एक बीज दिलं,
तर ती सुंदर, वाढतं-खेळतं, फलतं-फुलतं शिशु निर्माण करते,
कारण तीच निसर्ग आहे.
एक दिला तर दहा करून देणारी अशी निसर्ग-आई आहे.
तिच्या मुळे आपण आहोत,
आपल्या मुळे ती नाही.
जर स्वच्छ प्राणवायू नसेल तर
घराचा अन्नकोषच नसतो, जीवनच थांबतं.
आणि निर्मळ पाणी नसेल, तर
जीवनाचा श्वासही टिकू शकत नाही.
हा आपल्या प्रत्येक श्वास देवा चा
प्रतिनिधी आहे आणि जगत चा विश्वास निसर्ग आहे.

# Ti Pan Nisarg

Gharaala jar beej dila, tar sampoorn vasundharevar
Phulaanchi aani paanaanchi chaar-chaughi pasarte.
Strila jar ek beej dila,
Tar ti sundar, vaadhat-kheltat, phalat-phultat shishu cha nirmaan karte,
Kaaran tich nisarag aahe.
Ek dila tar daha karun denaali ashi nisarag-aai aahe.
Tichya mule aapan aahot,
Aaplya mule ti naahi.
Jar swachchh praanvaayu nasel tar
Gharaacha annkoshach nasto, jeevanach thaambta.
Aani nirmal paani nasel, tar
Jeevanacha shwaasahi tikoo shakat naahi.
Haa aaplya pratyek shwaas devaacha
Pratinidhi aahe aani jagat cha vishvaas nisarag aahe.

# मौन

जेव्हा मनाची हाक, हाताचा स्पर्श,
आणि शब्दांचे महत्व संपते,
तेव्हा मौन बोलते.
जेव्हा मेहनतीचा घाम सुकतो,
अवसंरचना दार बंद होतो,
आशाकिरणचा दिवा विझतो,
तेव्हा मौन बोलते.
जेव्हा विपरीत परिस्थितीचे वादळ
तांडव करते
आणि सत्ययांची सर्गम
आत्मा ऐकू शकत नाही,
तेव्हा मौन बोलते.
जेव्हा जबाबदाऱ्या आणि आपली स्वप्ने
यांच्या संघर्षात
स्वप्ने अकाल मृत्यू भरतात,
तेव्हा मौन बोलते.

जेव्हा एखादा मनुष्य
हास्याच्या मुखवट्याच्या मागे लपतो,
तेव्हा त्यांचे अस्थिर डोळे,
छातीवरची घडी घातलेले हात
आणि त्याच्या वेदनांचे मौन
खूप काही बोलत असते.
जेव्हा काळाच्या प्रचंड वादळात
मनुष्य ना वाकतो, ना कोसळतो,
तेव्हा त्याच्या ठाम उभेपणाचे मौन बोलते.

जेव्हा वर्षानुवर्षांचा विश्वास तुटतो,
तेव्हा अविश्वासाने जखम झालेल्या मनाचा
मूक हंबरडा, मौन बोलतो.
मनाच्या किंचाळण्यात मौन बोलते
जेव्हा जीवनाच्या धक्क्यानंतरही
आस्थेच्या खडकांवर उभे राहिलेले
घर टिकून राहते,
तेव्हा त्या आस्थेचे मौन
संपूर्ण ब्रह्मांडात बोलत असते.

# Maun

Jevha manachi haak, haataacha sparsh,
Aani shabdaancha mahatva sampate,
Tevha maun bolte.
Jevha mehnaticha ghaam sukto,
Avasanrachna daar band hoto,
Aashaakirancha diva vijhto,
Tevha maun bolte.
Jevha viparit paristhitiche vaadal
Taandav karte
Aani satyanchya sargam
Aatma aikoo shakat naahi,
Tevha maun bolte.
Jevha jababdari aani aapli swapne karaachya dwandvayuddhaat
Swapne akaal mrutyu paavtat,
Tevha maun bolte.

Jevha ekhda manushya
Haasyaachya mukhvaatyachya maage lapto,
Tevha tyaanche asthir dole,
Chativarchya ghadi ghaatlele haath
Aani tyaachya vedanaanche maun
Khoop kahi bolat aste.
Jevha kaalachya prachand vaadalat
Manushya na vaakto, na kosalto,
Tevha tyaachya thaam ubhepanache maun bolte.

Jevha varshaanuvrshaancha vishvaas tutto,
Tevha avishvaasaane jakham jhaalelya manacha
Mook hambarda, maun bolto.
Manachya kinchaalnyat maun bolte
Jevha jeevanaachya dhakkyanantarahi
Aasthechya khadkaanvar ubhe raahilele
Ghar tikoon raahate,
Tevha tya aastheche maun
Sampoorn brahmaandaat bolat aste.

# *Poems in Gujarati*

# માં

માનવી જીવનું મમર્, એ મા.
માનસમાં છુપાયેલી માનસાઈ, એ મા.
વસંત ઋતુની કોયલની કુહુકની હૂકમાં
જે મીઠાસ છે, એ મા.
આંબાના મોરલામાં, ચૈતર્ માસના ચૈતર્રી ગુલાબમાં,
સાવનની પહેલી પ્હારથી ઊઠતી ભીની-ભીની માટીની સુગંધમાં,
કડકતી વીજળી અને ગજર્તા મેઘની જુગલબંધીમાં;
શરદ ઋતુની ધરૂજતી ઠંડીમાં, મસાલેદાર ઉકાળામાં,
આવા હજારો અનુભવોમાં જે જીવનનો પથ શીખવાડે, એ અનુભૂતિ છે મા.
મા તો એ દુલર્ભ આશીવાર્દ છે,
જે ભગવાન પણ શોધતા હોય છે.
મા ની હાજરી, એ કવચ કે જેના પાસે બેઠેલું બાળક સમજે
કે હવે કોઈ બગ વણ એને ખાઈ નહી.
જીવનનું પેટકું રમકડું, સાથી, ગુરુ, અને જીવનનું છેલ્લું આસરો,
હેચાણી ચડપટ, મનના ઊછળતા સાગરનું સ્થિર કિનારો — એ મા છે.
મા છે તો બધું જ “મારું” છે,
નહી તો કોઈ પણ “મારું” નથી હોતું.

# Maa

Maanvi jeevnu marm, ae Maa.
Maansmaan chhupaayeli maansai, ae Maa.
Vasant ritu ni koyel ni kuhuk ni hook maa
Je mithaas chhe, ae Maa.
Aamba na morla maa, Chaitra maas na chaitri gulaab maa,
Saavan ni pehli phuhaar thi utthi bhini-bhini maati ni sugandh maa,
Kadakti vijdi ane garajta megh ni jugalbandi maa;
Sharad ritu ni dhurajti thand maa, masaledaar ukaada maa,
Avaa hazaaro anubhavo maa je jeevan no path seekhvaade, ae anubhuti chhe Maa.
Maa to ae durlabh aashirvaad chhe,
Je Bhagwaan pan shodhta hoy chhe.
Maa ni haajari, ae kavach chhe, jena paase baithelu baalak samjhe
Ke have koi pan baag ene khaai nahi.
Jeevan nu petku ramaksu, saathi, guru, ane jeevan nu chellu aasro,
Hechaani chadpat, mann na uchhalta saagar nu sthir kinaaro – ae Maa chhe.
Maa chhe to badhuj "maaru" chhe,
Nahi to koi pan "maaru" nathi hotu.

# હું શૂન્ય છું

હા, અંકમાં હું એ શૂન્ય છું,
જે ક્ષણમાં એક લાખને એક કરોડ બનાવે!
નિશિતમાં હું એ તિમિર છું,
જે આવતી ઉષાની કિરણોને શુભ સજાર્વે.
મહેનતમાં હું એ અંશ છું,
જે ગુમનામીના મૌનમાં લુપ્ત થઈ જાય;
અને પર્શંસા પામનારો આનંદ-તાંડવના નશામાં
મગ્ન કરી દે.
રંગોમાં હું શ્વેત છું,
જે લોહીની લાલિમા, આકાશની નીલિમા,
સૂયર્ના પીતાંબરને અને ધરતીની હરિયાળીને
વધારે નીખારે!
ગગનનો એ અંધકાર હું જ છું,
જેના કારણે નજરો ખીલેલા ચાંદને નિહારે.
માનવીના રુદનમાં હું રુંધાઉ છું,
જેથી ખુલ્લા શ્વાસની એ સુધા પામે.
જીવનના દુઃખોમાં હું એ અશ્રુબિંદુ છું,
જે હષર્ભરી સ્મિતનું સાચું મૂલ્ય શીખવાડે.
સમસ્ત સૃષ્ટિમાં હું એ નિરંતર, નિરાકાર અસ્તિત્વ છું —
જેટલું બીજાની જડવાઈ રહે, તેટલું ઉભારતું વ્યક્તિત્વ.
તમે મને અપનાવો કે નહી,
હું ન ઓછો છું કે ન વધારે.
તમે મને માનો કે મેલો કહો,
પણ મને નકારી તો નથી જ શકતા.

# Hu Shunya Chhu

Ha, ankomaa hu e shunya chhu,
je kshanmaa ek lakhne ek karod banaave!
Nishitmaa hum e timir chhu,
je aavati usha ni kiranone shubh sarjave.
Mehnatma hum e ansh chhu,
je gumnami naa maunmaa lupt thai jaay;
ane prashansa paamnarro aanand-tandav naa nashamaa
magn kari de.
Rangomaa hum shvet chhu,
je lohina lalima, aakash ni neelima,
surya naa pitambarne ane dharti ni hariyaaline
vadhare nikhaare!
Gagan no e andhakar hum j chhu,
jena kaarane najaro khilela chaandne nihaare.
Manvi naa rudanmaa hum rundhaum chhu,
jethi khulla svash ni ae sudha pame
Jeevan naa dukhomaa hum e ashrubindu chhu,
je harshbhari smitnu saachu moolya sikhvade.
Samast srushti maa hum e nirantar, nirakaar astitva chhu–
jetji bija ni jadvai rahe ubhartu vyaktitva. Tame mane apmavo
ke nahi, hu nathi ochu ke jaaju, tame mane maano ke melo,
pan mane nakaari toh naj sako.

# *Poems in English*

# Summer's Sojourn

Summer is here! Schools' shut!
Whole days and nights are playtime!
Cousins join in adding to the vacationing spirit of limitless laughter, fun and frolic.
Picnics along waterfalls or river banks.
Scrunchy, home made snacks are filled into wicker baskets.
Fresh fruits compete with large canisters of fresh juices.
Watermelons, tomatoes, mangoes juiced and curd churned into buttermilk all make for great refreshing and energizing drinks.
Trees laden heavy with their luscious gifts, entice young and old! Raw mango pickles.
The aroma of pungent, hot, smoky mustard oil wafting in the air.
Buttermilk dipped green chillies drying on thin sarees.
Broad wedges of carrots, okras, radishes and cluster beans, soaked in brine and turmeric water. All of them sun bathing on cotton sheets.
Mother Nature too seems to be in an expansive, revved mode.
She bursts into a riot of colours; sashaying down meadows, across all meridians.
The valley of wild flowers break into a merry dance, ignoring the heat.
Fields are lush with their treasures of bounty.
Snow peaks offer their life-giving streams, to sustain new growth on Earth.
Oceans roar with swelling waves, their strength renewed with replenished supply of water.

Sunrises and sunsets dazzle with unique hues.
Full of magic and uplifting emotions!
Way too endearing than the scorching, fiery daylight!

This poem was featured in the "Summer Sashays: Poetic Prose Piece" by The Soul Scribers Society.

# Soul's Stirrings

Far away the strong beacon of an extra tall, dark and
mysterious light house, kept beckoning!
From the horizon it looked like a large, one yellow-eyed, red
monster!
High tide set in, sending the waves to swell and leap!
The vast expanse of the ocean seemed foreboding and sinister!
But schedules, duties, responsibilities loomed above rationale
and reckoning!
Firmament, with its last residue of twilight hues was way too
deep purple, blue and ashen!
If we must set sail, then it must be now or else we will have
very few indicators of a shoreline!
For, a recent hurricane had rendered numerous villages along
the atoll, fragmented and flattened!
"All hands onboard, haul the anchor, hoot the foghorn thrice
and full steam ahead, North. Ahoy, Boy, Ahoy!".
This sharp call of the Captain, on the megaphone, broke the
trance of the novice sailor boy!
The Captain turned to go into the cabin, when he spotted the
three black cormorants.
Perched on the tallest mast of the lower deck, their bodies
silhouetted against the fading light's remnants!
He muttered a silent prayer and looked up at the rumbling,
ominous sky!
Further away, lightning flashed its electrifying claps across the
indigo canvas!
Swaying, dipping, massive waves crashing against his twenty
storey high cabin's front glass...

The Captain desperately held on to his internal balance, for the lurching ship was impossible to balance!
His precious cargo, of The Big Five Cats, a hundred in all, were being transferred, en masse!
To an Eden's Garden like an exclusive Island, with plenty of prey and shelter for these predators.
A safe sanctuary, in common parlance!
Then, like a miracle, the weather turned calm and equanimous.
Faint lights streaked the crescent horizon, it was daybreak on the shores.
A dawn rises in all its reassuring glory, in a manner most magnanimous!

This poem was featured in the "Soul Serenade Anthology collection of Poems, by The Soul Scribers Society, Salem."

# Childhood

The lush green meadows,
The hunter with bow and arrows.
Clusters of violets and roses
The butterflies hovering over them singing their praises.
Tall, strong pines, like some guard, they stand,
With wonder I look up at them, a bunch of flowers, in my hand.
Should I run between them pines,
Chasing that mischievous rabbit of mine?
Soft Earth tickles my toes,
The grass smiles at me, without minding my nudging toes.
While I splash through the puddle,
Trying to get across the hurdle.
Suddenly, a squirrel scurries, leaving her collection of corns, nuts & berries.
A parrot whisks away from his perch with a monkey in his pursuit.
These and other memories fleet b ,
On the mirror of the mind,
Leaving one to nostalgically sigh.
Wanting, once again, those blissful times of childhood to find!

# Success - What is it?

To a chrysalis emerging from its cocoon as a gorgeous butterfly, flitting around in a garden of roses... that is, success!
To a tiny, blind, jujube sized creature, latching onto its Mother's internal teat and emerging as a joey after 18 months, to prance and gambol on open meadows... that is, success!
To a seed thrusting its way from the dark bowels of Earth, to see the first ray of sunlight... that is, success!
To a singer, in a family of business tycoons, recording and selling chartbusters... that is, success!
To a drug addict or a phobic person to overcome personal demons and lead a fun-filled, fulfilling life... that is, success!
To a double-leg amputee scaling Mount Everest, running the Marathon... that is, success!
Success is not the social identity card of gold medals and first ranks in the report cards.
It is not only the material possessions and the innumerable zeros in the bank passbook.
It's your resilience, in the face of confidence, self-esteem and self-worth, blown to shards!
Success is nurturing a lifetime of friends, family and relations, not virtual followers on social hooks!

## Feel the Magic of Mother Nature!

See the magic of an ancient planet's ever new dawn, painted
on the canvas of an azure sky.
In hues of bright, soft pastels, watch the Golden Orb rise and
smile on the Earth.
Dazzling us with its perennial light filling our hearts with hope,
strength and joy of knowing Life's worth!
Inhale deep and feel the magic of moist earth, wet grass, dew
drops shimmering like rainbow coloured glass beads on
flowers and their delicate petals.
On the turquoise lake, glide innumerable pairs of both black
and white swans!
Chirping, squawking, trilling and warbling birds carry their
multi-hued, feathered canopy into the mountain high!
Chipmunks, meerkats and rabbits chatter standing on their
hind legs, on top of their mounds!
Guarding, signalling and warning each other of every threat!
Be it from predatory birds in the air or wolves and hounds on
the high grounds!
Robust pines, sturdy teaks, majestic mahogany, crisp ciders
and the strong scented sandalwood and earthy eucalyptus!
The forest is thick, deep, dark and mysterious!
The half-rotted seeds, berries, fruits, sticks and leaves,
All offer building materials, to create cosy homes for beavers,
weasels and platypus!
As the dusk approaches, every bird, bee and countless
inhabitants return to their distinct nest!
A lazy full moon smiles on this Earth, bathing us all in its
ethereal, silvery light!

Cicadas, crickets, frogs and all creatures nocturnal, sing their scintillating symphony, pierced by a loud hoot or a roar, as if to register a protest!
Fireflies flit about, lighting momentarily the shrouded forest!
Marvel at these creations of Mother Nature, wonder with awestruck wits and feel the warmth of this magic!

# Freedom

Dear bird flying so weightless on azure blue, take me too on
your wings, I want to soar up with you!
To see the lush meadows, sparkling brook, snow-capped
mountains, checkered fields and chimney tops coughing forth
grey fountains.
The distant lands I would like to visit,
Not just read and imagine them as I do here.
I would like to make new friends, for no mean or selfish ends.
With you, I would spring forth joy in a loving child.
With all my inhibitions shrugged off and nothing at all to hide.
With you, I would learn to weave deftly the nests,
On whose durability your family rests.
Dear bird, I wish I could come with you!
I know these are but wishful dreams, which will not come true
it seems!
But still you kindled a hope in me anew.
You have shown me the importance of freedom;
The value of mental freedom over a physical one!
Breaking chains of solitude and self-pity,
I shall reach out to the Sun!
Little bird, so small in stature, you are mighty in your wisdom.

# A Starlit Night

Dark, tall, checkered buildings.
Well pruned shrubs with overlapping creepers.
Long winding roads, frogs croaking and giving messages in codes.
All these and many beautiful sights we see, hear and enjoy on STARLIT nights!
On the deep blue sky appears a lazy crescent moon;
While the birds in their nests wait for the dawn to come soon.
When every tired worker slumbers soundly in his block,
A solitary soul you'll find by the sea shore,
Sitting lifeless on a huge rock,
Wishing for peace of mind and nothing more.
Gazing at the roaring and soaring waves of the stormy oceans,
Comparing them to the waves of depression,
Dashing against her already saddened heart!
Suddenly she looks up at the stars.
The bright lights and inspiring creations of Nature.
The shining ones representing the good opportunities of future,
And hoping sincerely that none of them are held behind ruthlessness' bars!
The noisy and mocking city she shuns,
That is why she is here, holding calmness within darkness that stuns.

# Pouring Rain, Steaming Coffee!

Tip, tap drops and pours the rain; down it drops and pours
into the roofs of houses and trains!
The people rushing for their work have very early their oats;
Kids come out on the door steps, make and sail their paper
boats!
It was a dazzling morning; it had just stopped raining and the
sun suddenly smiled, spreading its golden tresses!
A whistling wind occasionally reminded one of the
thunderous, pouring days!
Sitting in the veranda feeding birds and a squirrel; my eyes
scanned the nearby hillocks covered in a green mattress!
For the fish waits on one leg the crane,
Out of the den, come and crawl the snails!
The frogs chatter unrhymically in the night!
The couples and children, old and young, cuddle themselves
warm and tight !
Sipping aromatic, hot filter coffee, penning lines to my darling,
who has been sailing the seas for 90 days!
Early in the morning a large bouquet of orange tulips arrived
with my darling's note!
It read, "Crossing  choppy oceans near Corsica, missing you!
These Tulips carry my sense of longing, for it's this yearning
that they denote!"
Tulips, our favourite flowers, because of two lips and orange,
a colour both of us revel in; it exudes exuberance!
Miles apart, yet fused in thought, fond memories and
remembrance!
The shower, after the Autumn to dry our wet brains!

This poem was featured in an online anthology by Rhyvers Press.

# Girl, I Love That!

Girl, down the Eons, through Times' ever spinning wheels,
you have remained tensile and diligent!
Like the sky, sun and moon, who are too ancient to even
count the years; come out each morning, noon and night in a
form ever so new and different.
Girl, I love that,
Like these elements you are constantly connected to your
core, yet are adept at adapting to changing miles, thus being
self-sufficient!
Down the stairwell of centuries, you Sita, Draupadi, Heer,
Razia and any woman, have been hedged in by fences of
hierarchy, patriarchy, rituals, homemaking and traditions!
Punished and marginalised for being frank and fearless!
Girl, I love that,
Like a tiny brook or rivulet, you keep flowing despite
innumerable hindrances!
Girl, you were born as a Life form, not a gender!
These societal gender benders will never tire of clipping your
wings!
Girl, I love that,
Like the surfy edges of a breaking wave, even as it recedes
from the shoreline, you grow wings and soaring even higher...
above the powder puff clouds of the thermal winds!
When your spouse snatches away your child,
When your boss takes all the credit for your efforts,
When the building contractor renders you homeless, From
the roof you're labouring to construct,
When the school authorities rob you of your basic education,
you don't fade into oblivion!

Girl! I love that,
You managed to find a guide, support or beacon from a crowd of unknowns.
Even when those so called "YOURS" are hell bent on being stranger than strangers!
Burnt with acid, brutally raped, forcefully aborted, killed as an infant; pushed into prostitution, at an age when you don't even know what this curse is!
The list of atrocities against you is endless.
Not just physical scars, but emotional, mental, psychological, & economical are inflicted upon you.
Yet, Girl, your spirit is boundless!
Society may mar or maul you,
Belittle you for your success, crucify you for your individuality, ostracise you for your steel guts and outspokenness!
But, Girl, I love you for your instinct to survive, is much stronger than that to sever!
I love that the human soul continues to shine on long after the bodily form is gone.
I love that to love anything, the very thread of Life is to be alive to that moment's eternal experience!

# Learn, But Not from Books Alone!

Learning, like growing, is an ever evolving process!
Learn, not just from books, but from an ever flowing river,
over boulders and terrain rough!
That these natural obstacles serve to filter debris of impurities
and give crystal clear water in excess!
So also, hindrances in our life journey's path make us focused,
better prepared and tough!
Learn from a nursing Mother elephant, in the pitch black
night, feeding an orphaned fawns, or a mother dog nursing an
abandoned kitten at dawn!.
This divine lesson of caring, nurturing and compassion, is
priceless to us humans who mostly group together on grounds
of, "useful connections"
Learn from a flitting butterfly the precious importance of
freedom and the joys of adventurous spirit!
Never lose the inner Innocence of a curious childlike mind;
Overlaying it with norms, trends, jargons and everything
derelict,
Due to the taxing routines and relentless onslaught of our
existence's grind!
In the University of Life, when the Teacher called Reality,
turns the pages of Experiences,
Then Introspections, Realisation, and Knowledge create a
tapestry of circumstances,
That mirrors Truth in its raw, ruthless and radiant form!
Learn all the subjects and languages created by humans,
studying all that is on the Earth and beyond!
But, never forget to practice the language of Humanity,
Whether in calm weather or storm!
For, remember, the more Elixir you draw from Joy's pond,
the more rejuvenation it unbound!

# Fiery Mirage

A childhood spent chasing parrots away from ripe guavas and grapes.
Rolling an old tire down dusty street.
Running after the festive, colourfully decorated elephants, in brass artefacts, emblazoned silk sheets.
Draped in huge scarves with buntings, laces, brass bells and figurines of different shapes.
Lazy afternoons spent day dreaming and watching the clouds create stories in the sky!
Galloping up a tiny hillock on a moonlight night,
To marvel at the shimmering lake.
Listening to the symphony of cicadas, crickets and frogs!
Tall, ghostly sentinels of Cyprus, pines, spruced eucalyptus, stand guard to this treasure trove!
Behold, on the opposite side a molten silver cascade covered with millions of darting fireflies, a magical sight.
Youth gives boundless imagination, mobility, freedom and a sense of coming of age.
So then, did the eyes play tricks, peering through a screen of fog?
Or were these milky falls, just a Fiery Mirage?
Those blessed days of Youth emanate as smoke from the chimney of existence, above the furnace of reality and evaporated into the firmament high!

# My Dearest Heartbeats, A Mother's Musings

My dearest darlings, from the first kick I felt in my womb,
To the moment I held you in my arms;
It was a living blessing of transforming from a life from walking this planet to bringing other new lives to Earth!
Yes, there were innumerable aches and pains,
But forever all the times and seasons; whether spring, summer or rains;
Changed, to a new hue and colour, just by your Birth!
Like one never knows the exact moment of glory of a blooming flower,
So too your milestones were Big Surprises!
Your first gurgles, your first eye contact, your first words, were all dazzling beams of Sunrises!
Just your presence demanded and commanded that all movements, any outings, every activity were in tune with your divine and so full of Innocence's Power!
My darlings, may this world be a better place for you to walk on this vibrant terra firma!
May Life bestow upon you the fortitude to tide over;
Both good times and bad!
Don't dance on your head when all goes your way,
Nor when situations are dire, feel bogged down and sad!
Long after I am gone, I know my darlings, I will still be walking this Earth, through You...
For you are my flesh and blood, carrying on my legacy, touching lives, be they many or few!

# I Met You on Instagram

The first time I saw your fleeting smile and the brown curtain
of your curly sweep past those honey brown eyes,
My heart held that breath, when I beheld this glowing sight!
We connected instantly, chatting into the wee hours of the
night...
Myriad topics we found to discuss, thrash out, mock, argue;
simply unwilling to say our goodbyes.
At times we would both never realise the lapse of time,
beholding the breaking dawn's sight!
The Universe conspired to amalgamate us in an incredible
moment.
Long before we met in person, we were best friends, life
partners, and soul mates on Instagram!
My prayer to the Powers that be is that our Life's journey be
momentous,
Where we become each other's inspiration and shun all things
sham!

# Closed Door

It's time to dust the files one last time!
It's that juncture when this ticking wall clock, fluttering calendar and the cold, steel bell will give me the final smile.
Tomorrow, there will be no rush for a train at 7 A.M...
No more wiping the mahogany chairs and tables, balustrades and the arched window frames with stained glass!
From tomorrow there will be no jurisdictions,
"My Lord's" or binding schedules of A.M' s & P.M' s!
For tomorrow I will be home, away from this magnificent court,
Chattering crowds, crockery and clinking glasses!
Tomorrow these hallowed portals and their intricately carved doors will be closed for me forever...
Today I leave to never return!

# The Day My Faith Was Shaken

A new day has dawned, with a promise of a smiling sun
renewed!
The air is thick with Ambrosia fragrance of exotic flowers'
dew.
The birds are singing their choral symphony for which
listeners are few.
I was cycling along the yellow lighted, jaundiced, quiet road,
Felt the cool breeze pat my cheeks.
Suddenly, I heard tires screeching ahead of me !
A large bundle was dumped with a sickening thud on the
roadside!
I raced ahead, but the car zoomed away, leaving a half-
crushed face on the kerbside!
It was the lifeless form of a well-known journalist!
His Truth cost him too dear
He was another voice silenced in the many Braveheart's long
list!
This morning is the day my Faith is badly shaken!

# Love Will Find You

In medieval times knights impressed damsels with shining armours, Arabian steeds, castles and precious jewels.
The present times 'Heroes', woo their dames with cars, bank balances, spunky accessories, swanky abodes and watches that are bejewelled!
Friends become paramours...
Paramours become soulmates...
But, sometimes, an alliance breaks just before marriage!
Leaving the hapless Bride and Groom to rue and mourn!
Leave it dear heart, let the Bird of Love fly!
If it's to become yours, it will come back to you!
Bringing joy to you and your family!
Love, if destined will find You!

## Dance

Dance to the pulsating heart beat!
Dance to set free all your hidden feelings!
Dance till you vibrate to an exalted frequency; right from the crown of your head to your toes on your feet!
Dance like there is none, yet every atom is, with you from the surroundings!
Dance to the rhythm of seasons, the rise and fall of waves!
Dance to the tumultuous roaring of cascades, to the whispers of ripples, in the pond beneath!
Dance to the murmuring silence of the depths of oceans!
Dance to the rustle of the pathways that the current paves!
Dance to the whistling leaves, to the piercing flute call of bamboo forests!
Dance to the orchestra of warbling birds and chirping fledglings in nests!
Each movement releasing into the Universe, scattered across galaxies!
Clearing all internal complexities and perplexities!
A saga of sheer joy, bliss and exuberance!
An emotion, an experience, a story, a verse... echoing through the cosmos with its ecstatic reverberance!

# Mask

Like The Bard mentioned, in his famous lines,
"All the World's a stage and we are mere characters!"
All of us role play, many a times!
Very subtle maybe, but we drop strong hints of dislike,
disagreement, discontent and all 'dis' with a smiley mask!
Many times, one wears a mask of "All Izz Well" when
everything inside us is falling apart!
At work, in a house, at a construction site, or any tough task,
demands that one should wear the mask of a stoic;
setting all our difficulties to depart!
Big pixie eared, large eye-lashed blue- eyed masks, with
painted rosy cheeks and an enlarged smile,
Dissipate all worries and bring back a happy smile on young
and old alike!
Dear friends, the question is, will these masks take away our
core self?

# April Fool's!

Some say April Fool's Day has different origins and meanings!
Some say when the citizens did not know the change of
calendar from the Gregorian to the present form,
They were hailed as April Fool's as a norm!
Some say it is mentioned in Chaucer's Canterbury Tales as a
tradition of innocent pranks and other leanings!
Whatever may or may not be the source of this fun-filled day,
pet's enjoy a day of mirthful banter and a year full of happy
laughter,
Why segregate just a day for joy?
Let's make it a festival of a lifetime...
Life is a gift, a blessing; come let's celebrate it!

# Potter

A Potter spins the wheel to create magic from a ball of putty clay
A fine agleam of art, artistry. skill and artisanship is the potter.
Admired by one and all, rich and poor,
Children, people of all ages, even a mad hatter,
Soft dry Earth blowing in the wind stings the eyes;
But, in the hands of a Potter, new wondrous forms it takes, enthralling the beholder's eyes!
This wheel of the Potter is akin to the wheel of Time;
And our life cycle is his making and breaking of creations.
For, from dust we rise and go back to dust,
Carrying with us, all our glories and limitations!

# Sunday

Sun, Sunny, Sunday!
Rise and shine folks!
It's a day to discover new shops,
Addas, art galleries and old places renovated with new looks!
When you connect with old friends and new,
Chart new terrains, full of intrigue, it becomes a fun day!
Whether you pursue hobbies, jobs or fill your days with chores mundane!
It becomes a blessing, when days begin or end with laughter ringing in the air.
Mugs of hot tea and coffee clinking, pets running amok; be they pompons, rottweilers, golden retrievers or great Danes!
Friends, like families, form a bulwark against stressful situations.
For this 'SHIP' of friendship, weather's all storms of Life's ups and downs; including unpredictable circumstances!
All relationships, running on the fuel of care, share and honesty.
Come let us rejoice each day and make it sweet with smiles, tangy, spice and mirthful minty!

# I Am A Sapphire Gatherer

"Who art thou, O Mysterious one?
Like you I've seen none.
What brings thee to these desolate shores?
Daring the bitter cold and foot sores?"

"People gather jewels but I, I gather Sapphire.
People burn hearths, but I, I burn to kindle my fire.
People hoard priced oaks and teaks, but I collect dead driftwood!
People host banquets but I, I feast or dine according to the weather's mood."

"Why is it that some get all they want;
While others die of every kind of want?
Why is it that some souls soar high;
While others sink into the murky waters of tears and sigh?
Why is it that dreams come true,
Only to fade and leave a faint memory?"
"It is not the poverty of wealth that kills; It is that of compassion that sets the grinding mills.
It is not the lack of food or clothes that one feels;
But the death of human understanding kills.
Why is it that some are made to smoulder like embers;
And yet others are frozen by ages of loneliness.?
Why this disparity and gaping chasm, that deepens like the sea by every fathom?"

"Can you answer, O Stranger?"

"I'm but a ghost of dead hopes; of a soul who in the alleys of despair, gropes!
It is true, for reality is hard-hitting and stranger than a stranger!"

# Dusk

Adorning a fiery dress she leaves; putting to sleep all mankind, birds and leaves!
She is gentle, majestic and exudes radiant light,
She is the joyful, sad, enchanting Twilight!
She enters the golden pool of silvery waves,
To reach her abode of pearls that oyster saves!
High above a solitary bird bids farewell;
To the elms swaying as if in a dance of farewell.
Night crowds around like a velvet blanket.
Shrouding the bright waters in a black net.
But still one amber sparkles, lingering to stay, with the world in which it revels!
Far away a bell chimes; infusing a sense of infinite calm.
The voice of Lord's praise sung in rhymes, arises from the Earth around, reaching Heaven through this calm.
Another day has ended...
With all its swords and songs,
Yet, for some delight or consolation one longs.
Many dreams seem to have been buried,
In the toil for fulfilling basic needs.
Yet, one, awaits the rejuvenating dawn,
When we can sail the ocean of Life, like a swan.
The dawn that gives priceless hope;
Hope, that Despair will not throttle like a gnarled rope;
That, a soul in alleys of Loneliness and Tears need not grope!

This poem was featured in an online magazine, "Kabita Live, Platform for Poets."

## Death, The Eternal Flow

Life is so unpredictable and fragile,
But, the glinting soap-bubbly Ego is so strong, dexterous and agile.
It convinces us that the risen sun will not set without our permission!
We, unaware beings, think this as solid reality rather than an illusion!
Death, on the other hand is a moonbeam of a calm mind,
Trapped, in the pithy, pitch black mesh of separation.
Death is a fountain of ideas polluted by filthy effluents of hypocrisy and suppression...
Death is the immense loneliness of an abandoned elder parent or pet without fangs...
The scorching eyes of these burning souls, searching for their own, who are long gone!
Death is the final release of all shackles, of rituals, shallow practices and jugular jargons!
Death is the massive heaving of a heart breathing Freedom!
The Spirit spreads its wings to glide into a blissful Kingdom!

# Pappa's Princess

A Father they say, is the solid, secure fortress and roof of a House...
A Mother, it is said, is the super glue that holds the bricks together and makes it a Home...
A Son, it is said, is the answer to all the prayers of lasting camaraderie, everlasting support and fulfilling promises;
A Daughter, on the other hand is Nature's blessing, where scented flowers, chirping birds, gurgling brooks and starry nights; descend on this planet to re-home!
Her bumbling attempt at speech is transformed into something meaningful!
Her every stumbling step is twinkle toed and beautiful...
Her presence lights the days with radiant sunshine!
Nights are wakeful and taxing; yet her one smile is, so soothing as the mellow moonshine!
She brings so much fun, imparting and taking Life lessons, which are so enduring and graceful.
On Pappa's shoulders the world seems so wonderful, obstacles pulverised to dust!
With Pappa every toy, balloon and dress is mine; all treasure troves seem to be in my fist!
My chant, "My Pappa strongest, my Pappa endearing, my Pappa is the best!"
For, when he holds my hand and gives a reassuring smile; all doubts seem to rest!
He is my Hero and I am his Princess;
this spot for any Prince, I will not relinquish!

## Space

Immeasurable, vast, limitless expanse, is what one fathoms as space.
No matter how many galaxies, milky ways, asteroids and meteors one estimates;
Our one tiny speck of a planet Earth is what we know as a habitable place!
Just as the planets hum their own orbital song, without colliding with their other mates;
So too we humans need to learn this precious lesson of live and let live!
To give enough space to one's partner, colleague, friend or any individual to grow and thrive, not just survive!
For, after all we too imbibe in us this stardust...
Therefore, as a species we are born to grow, evolve and flourish without going bust!

# Eyes

These immense pools of intense emotions...
Reflect a lifetime of shifting moments, situations and relations,
A starry-eyed youth's stare, turns into the steely gaze of
beleaguered, weary middle-aged person.
Misty, cataract shrouded eyes, keep waiting for the fledglings
to return this season!
Searching, through a grey curtain of weak health, lost loved
ones and innumerable goals,
These eyes keep smiling through all weathers.
They learn to make new connections, whether human, furred
or with feathers,
For, eyes are indeed the windows of our souls!
Keeping hope alive, in rough circumstances, torn confidence
and shattered self-esteem,
Holding on till the glorious sun of success...
Time beholds!
Where the fountain of Joy overflows into blissfulness' stream!

# The Unstruck Melody - Anhad Naad

Wafting on the Zephyros winds of spring, reverberated the piercing call of a flute,
Heralding the times of bounty and good cheer.
Fruits bursting on every branch of multifarious trees!
Where deer, tigresses, giraffes, lionesses all tend to their new born and co-exist without fear!
Birds busy building their nests;
While singing their merry ditty, traa-a-la-la-ding-a-ling-ling!!
The sunny fairy with her diaphanous tiny wings splashed a few drops of sunshine, and sunflowers, daisies and daffodils smiled!
The Moony fairy took a few dew drops, some strands of moonlight, a bit of azure and dotted the Earth...
Irises, Morning glories and Forget-me-nots, sprung up with a giggling sound of their mirth!
Dusk cherubs borrowed many hues from the setting Sun; flitted around the lake's edges, while playing their harps!
Flowers blossomed into a rich tapestry of colours, carpeting every inch of the fertile land and steep escarpments!
Our dreams too are probably made of such phantasmagorical sights!
Subconscious thoughts, projecting scenes of calm, joy, betrayal and frights!
When the mind reaches a state of stillness.
Where the cosmos hums a primordial AUM, going beyond all soundlessness.
This soundlessness is the state of our inner conscious self!
An unstruck melody of infinity, with no beginnings or end, no rapturous compositions ringing out,

Beyond all emotions, memories and pains; just a core
connection of bliss, emanates from the depth of Oneself!
Far from the maddening crowds, half-truths and abuses
shattered all around and about,
Just this all enveloping, frictionless, White Noise...
Our Soul descends into a silvery pool of immense grace and
poise.
White swans glide silently on these placid waters.
Singing their Hamsa Geetham in Hamsadhvani...
Lulling the Universe into a deep stupor of awakened
awareness!
For these celestial vibrations are panacea for all maladies and
madness!
These sounds of perennial unstuck melody of resilience, help
us sail on Life's choppy oceans of cacophony... to the shores
of limitless Silence!

This poem was featured in the "Soul Song" Anthology collection of Poems, by The Soul Scribers Society.

# Une Nuit Blanche - A White Night!

The dappled, motley carpet of the Earth,
Vibrant with red, orange, dull gold maple leaves and half-
crushed flowers of myriad hues...
Heralding the passing of Autumn and the onset of frosty
winters the season of Birth!
Hibernating, pregnant, Polar Bear moms go as deep into
snow-bound caves, as permitted by their wide girth,
Mooses, deer, reindeer, and ermine foxes find shelter in
massive trunks,
Overlaid with creepers, lichens and velvety moss.
Protected from the Great Freeze, life is born as fawns, cubs,
colts, ewes and elephants with floppy trunks!
Mother Nature,
provides nuts, berries and seeds, which the squirrel saves;
Long before the hailstorm and blizzards leave their
fingerprints, dipped in silvery, driven snow, being embossed!
Cribs of Nativity scenes adorn every habitat!
Be they homes, malls, offices, shops or churches.
Tall trees, bereft of any growth, stand like sentinels facing the
bombardment of the Snow Flaky Army's march!
The air is thick with joyous bells proclaiming the Yuletide,
When the devout, both poor and rich, sing carols and gather
in great multitude,
Faith reigns supreme with heads bowed in prayer, kneeling on
the mahogany pews.
People, go about their paces, bracing themselves,
With thick fur coats, woollen socks, mittens, skullcaps, berets
and gumboots!

Rushing to and fro, from work or strolling the streets admiring the lovely wares exhibited on glass shelves.
The entire hemisphere seems to dazzle in a white sheath!
So charming, yet deep ravines, frozen lakes and fast flowing rivers can be lethal,
Bone-crushing phenomenon that to our planet, this winter bequests, can be dealt with, coped with, managed to a large extent.
How, oh, how, does one close the chasm of loneliness and hearts' growing distance?
Of apathy, indifference and frigid, dagger-like silence, between a once loving pair!
When the reaching out stops, the call of a heart falls on lost, hoary musings!
When this winter does not thaw into a spring of smiles, winks and warm embraces,
Then it's a never-ending Nuit Blanche, a sleepless, long, White Night!
With embers of hope and revival blown to smithereens, of tattered but tethered traces of trust; a shattering sight!

This poem was featured in the anthology, "Winterful Whispers," of the Yercaud Poetry Festival, 2023.

# Rainbow of Love

Blue, a colour one strongly connects to the vast firmament,
To the deepest, magnificent oceans,
Like the fathomless loyalty and love of siblings.
Red, the barometer of passion of lovers' blessings,
A choice made with wide-eyed delight,
to seal a feeling which is permanent.
Yellow, for comrades and friends who rejoice or reinforce,
When sunny times smile upon us, changing life's course.
Or thunderous clouds of dire circumstances and dried up resources.
Orange, a happy amalgam of co-existing
generations of family;
Where experience and youth,
Leader and follower, cohabit exceptionally.
Love of an artist for the art form that they showcase...
A writer's love for the written word which is precise...
Farmers tilling land or a champion chasing a cause...
Are all forms of love that persist, without a pause.
Like the purposeful flight of a dove to reach its mate,
So too a pet's love is incomparable, no matter what its fate!
Ambitions and aspirations are fuelled by
ceaseless love of goals;
Love, like life, has innumerable shades
Of hues and illuminating lessons.
Where there is care and share,
Love blooms into a multi-layered marvellous, lily,
With its warm fragrance and fuzzy heart laid bare.
All shades of love make you snivel, smile and giggle
At anything, be it heartfelt, heart wrenching or silly!

This poem was featured in an anthology, "An Anthology of Love - Shades of Love," 2022.

# Amber Autumn

Ochre, sun-tanned leaves fall on terra firma in a pell-mell fashion! Covering Mother Earth in its golden threads of Maple, Gulmohar, Eucalyptus, and many more! All the trees seem to be in unison, shedding their previous Spring's beautiful auburn robes. Nature adorns thick blankets of impermeable resin and moss, bracing itself to navigate the tightening grip of winter!

Squirrels, rodents, birds, and all creatures small and big collect their supply of food, feathers, and foliage. Mother Bears with their cubs, Big Cats with their offsprings, and innumerable species of other animals create their shelters. Deep hollow trunks of fallen trees, caves, and grottos, chiselled on the flanks of hillocks, all make for prime habitats. They line them with straw, cotton fluffs, plucked tendrils of creepers, and board them with sharp thistles. The air sharpens its raspy saw-like teeth to create a whistling symphony. Lakes sparkle in a rice-sheet-like veil on the surfaces while their waters still keep dancing beneath!

Meandering brooks and gushing waterfalls defy the murmurs of Autumn while singing their gurgling choruses! An Elixir called Life goes into deep sleep, in Autumn. Maybe because the Elements need to re-calibrate, recharge, and rejuvenate! They too need to catch their breath after working hard to create three seasons. The entire Planet buckles itself against the onslaught of the fast-approaching tough winter... Only to burst out radiantly in the next Spring!

The fifties and sixties of a human's life are the Autumn of our Earthly journey. A time to pause, take stock, and reflect. Rejoice without any regrets and celebrate the path travelled thus far! Partaking in the rejuvenating ambrosia of a rich motley of fulfilling experiences. Spending the remaining time with lots of good cheer, health, and equanimity. Then we surrender, at the very end, to our winter... which encases us in the Eternity of a never-ending slumber!

This poem was featured in the anthology, "Auburn Ambrosia" of the Yercaud Poetry Festival (2024), Soul Series of Soul Scribers Society.